THE BLUEPRINT

'THE MESSIAH'

God's Transcendent Plan of Redemption!

Faith Marie Baczko

A Song of Ascents. Of David

"I rejoiced with those who said to me,
"Let us go to the house of the LORD."
Our feet are standing in your gates, O Jerusalem.
Jerusalem is built like a city that is
closely compacted together [*united in fellowship*].
That is where the tribes go up, the tribes of the LORD,
To praise the name of the LORD
According to the statute given to Israel.
There the thrones for judgment stand,
The thrones of the house of David.
Pray for the peace of Jerusalem:
"May those who love you be secure.
May there be peace within your walls and security within your citadels."
For the sake of my brothers and friends, I will say, "Peace be within you."
For the sake of the house of the LORD our God,
I will seek your prosperity."
Psalm 122 NIV

The Blueprint

The Yahweh's House Series is dedicated to my precious son

Jesse Jordan Robinson.

Both Jesse and I have paid the tremendous cost of birthing this work

In the refining fire of God's Love.

Jesse died on September 10th 2006 in a fatal car accident.

He was twenty- four years old.

The fruit of this Ministry is accredited to Jesse as his inheritance in Christ.

The Blueprint

This series is a tribute to:

My Heavenly Father, the One to whom I have always been able to run to, pour out my heart every day, and receive nothing in return but love. I offer this work back to You Father as a sacrifice of love to be used in the fulfilment of Your plans and purposes.

To Jesus my LORD, my King and Lover of my soul—the One who made it all possible by His precious Blood. Your face is the face I long to see. May these works glorify Your great Name and bring You honour wherever they are taught. Blessing, Honour, Glory and Power belong to You alone forever and ever for You alone are worthy.

To the most precious Holy Spirit I have no adequate words to describe to depth of gratitude in my heart for You. You have been my Teacher and my Friend during the times I felt alone, my Comforter through the painful times; the One who gently and lovingly encouraged me to keep going when I wanted to quit, and who picked me up and carried me when I could not stand. I do not know how to express how much I love You, but I thank You from the very depths of my heart.

Yahweh's House Series

Acknowledgements

I wish to thank my Pastors Steve and Sandra Long for their encouragement and support, and for being true reflections of God's love. Thank you being a wonderful example of what it means to be Pastors of God's sons and daughters, and the great example you both are to the Body of Christ of what great leadership looks like.

I would like to thank Juanita Lubin for her friendship, support and her time spent with me to deal with the issues of my heart.

I would also like to thank Ann Reid, Caroline Phillips and Judy Wilson for being good friends when I needed friends, and for persevering in our friendship.

The Blueprint

© Copyright 2011—Faith Marie Baczko

Headstone Publishing
1-312 Reynolds St. Oakville Ontario L6J 3L8

All rights reserved

This book is protected by the copyright laws of Canada.

This book may not be copied or reprinted for commercial gain or profit.

This book or portions thereof may not be reproduced stored in a retrieval system or transmitted in any form without prior written permission of the publisher.

Unless otherwise identified, Scripture quotations are from the New King James Version, copyright ©1982 by Thomas Nelson, Inc.

Scripture quotations marked AMP are from the Amplified Bible. Old Testament copyright© 1965,1978 by Zondervan Corporation. The Amplified New Testament copyright© 1954, 1958, 1987 by the Lockman Foundation.

Scripture quotations marked NIV are from the HOLY BIBLE, NEW INTERNATIONAL VERSION Copyright © 1973, 1978, 1984 by International Bible Society. Used by permission of Zondervan Publishing House. All rights reserved.

Scripture quotations marked JNT are from the Jewish New Testament

copyright© 1979,1989,1990 by David H. Stearns Jewish New Testament Publications

ISBN:-13:978-1456585723

Email: contact@headstoneministries.ca

Website: www.headstoneministries.ca

Yahweh's House Series

CONTENT

FOREWORD	9
INTRODUCTION	11
SECTION I – A NEW MAN	15
A new Beginning in a New Land	17
The Promised Land – A New Man in the New Land	19
Jerusalem – God establishes His Throne in the New Land	21
SECTION II – THE FOUNDATION STONE	23
The Father Lays the Foundation Stone of His Temple	25
Israel is Established in the New Land as a Nation	27
The Passover Lamb is Sacrificed	29
SECTION III – THE CORNERSTONE	33
The Superstructure	35
The Holy Spirit Breathes Life into the Structure	39
The Gentiles are invited to enter	43
SECTION IV – THE HEADSTONE	47
The Body Grows up to the Head	49
The Headstone Completed in Christ	53
SECTION V – ONE NEW MAN	57
The One New Man is Birthed	59
Jesus - The Plumb Line	63
Zion – The Seat of the Government of God is Established	67
The Government Shall be upon His Shoulder	71
SECTION VI – THE BRIDE OF CHRIST	73
The Bride is Presented	75
Israel honored in Eternity	79
God's Everlasting Covenant with Israel	81
Honoring the Fathers	87
One United	95

The Blueprint – Foreword

The Blueprint,

Is also dedicated to the Jewish people

In honour of the nation of Israel;

The crucible in which God has chosen to

Fashion a Body,

Conformed to His Son, Jeshua,

The Hope of Israel, the Desire of all Nations,

To Glorify His Great name in the Heavens and the Earth.

FOREWORD

The Blueprint is the second manual in the series 'Yahweh's House'. Each work represents a facet of the House of God important to its completion. There are many important features of the early Church presently being restored, as God brings fresh revelation on key doctrines—all working to prepare the Body of Christ for great moves of God on the horizon. Every work that God has birthed in the past or is presently birthing, to enhance the building work of His House are all important to the completion of His House—each contributes its 'part,' *"For we know in part and we prophesy in part" (1Cor. 13:9).*

The measure that the House of God is structured according to the measure of the Father's design—whether individually or corporately—*determines the measure of His Glory it will reflect.*

> *"In Him the whole structure is joined (bound, welded together harmoniously, and it continues to rise (grow, increase) into a holy temple in the Lord [a sanctuary dedicated, consecrated, and sacred to the presence of the Lord]." Ephesians 2:21 AMP*

God has been at work over time, building His House, precept upon precept, according to the Body's ability to appropriate and process revelation. With the Body's apprehension of revelation and truth, and a grasp of its identity as *one being* conformed to the very image of Christ, comes the level of Glory it will appropriate—during this process the Body is continually moving from one level of the Glory of God to another.

The Blueprint — Foreword

Each work in this series represents significant features of the end-time Temple or House of God—referred to as *The Headstone* in the series. The intent of the *Yahweh's House Series* is to bring understanding of important facets of the Headstone, such as Israel and women, each being a vital component to the completion of the House *the Father designed* to house His Presence, and carry the fullness of His Glory. The completion of *The Headstone* and the release of a company of Headstone people will be important for preparing the way of the coming of the Lord. *If we build what He is building, He will return to fill it!*

The Headstone is the culmination of four thousand years of God's work (beginning with Abraham) refined and perfected in the last days in a body of servants. The building of the Headstone is established and purposed to come forth in the Power and might of the Holy Spirit, in the timing of the apostolic age—the final stage of the building of God's Temple.

The Headstone will reflect the whole counsel of God and be filled with all the fullness of God in order to carry the weight of His Glory that will cover the earth, "*...and he shall bring forth the headstone thereof with shoutings, crying, Grace, grace unto it*" *(Zech.4-7 KJV).*

Faith Marie Baczko

INTRODUCTION

"Every valley shall be exalted And every mountain and hill brought low; The crooked places shall be made straight And the rough places smooth; the glory of the LORD shall be revealed, and all flesh shall see it together; for the mouth of the LORD has spoken." Isaiah 40:4-5

The Bride prepared for the coming of the Bridegroom is without spot or wrinkle. As the return of the King draws near, God will ensure that His House is established according to His Blueprint, cleansed and set in order to host His Presence. The Lord is a consuming Fire, faith and obedience are therefore the virtues on which the foundation of His sanctuary is constructed in order to sustain the weight of His Glory that is coming.

God's Holy Sanctuary, His Throne of justice and His Seat of mercy can only be fashioned by the Lord. However, God chooses to demonstrate His strength and establish His plans through a people of faith conformed to His image. These are His sons and daughters who walk in the attributes of righteousness, justice and mercy, who carry His anointing, His authority and exude His fragrance.

John the Baptist was such a man, prepared by God to, *"Prepare the way of the Lord"* for His first coming. John was a chosen instrument through whom God worked to prepare the heart of Israel and cleanse it through repentance from sin and dead works. As we approach the time of His *second coming*, the preparation remains the same—*repentance of sin and our dead works carried out in the flesh apart from the direction of the Holy Spirit.*

The Blueprint – Introduction

God is calling a forerunner people to work with Him to prepare the way for the re-entrance of the King of Glory unto planet earth. As we repent of our dead works, we will then be able to perceive and understand His plans, and the blueprint of the sanctuary to which He will return.

God's Blueprint is *Jeshua*! All that He is—His mind, His heart, His attributes, His attitude, His ways and *His chosen form* as the Son and the Root of Israel—is the Plumb Line of the House of God! Sadly, many have committed great atrocities in Jesus' name, and sadly, both Israel and the world have judged Jesus and Christianity by those who claim to follow Him, rather than allowing His Words and His ways to judge those who make claims to His Name.

> *"...Yes, the time is coming that whoever kills you will think that he offers God service. And these things they will do to you because they have not known the Father nor Me." John 16:3*

The Blueprint portrays God's unfolding plan of the House He has been at work building over the centuries; a House where He will dwell with man in eternity. The building work began in Israel, and as the Gentile nations are grafted in, it is completed in Israel.

> *"Then the word of the LORD came to me: "The hands of Zerubbabel have laid the foundation of this temple; his hands will also complete it." Zechariah 4:8-9 NIV*

God has promised in His Word that He will make out of two—the Jewish people and Gentile Christians—one New Man, a New Man that is to become the eternal Dwelling place of God. *The Blueprint* reveals the incredible story

The Blueprint – Introduction

of God's plan to bring about this seemingly impossible dream. The plan begins with Abraham, and as it unfolds over history, reveals the detailed Blueprint of the awesome Edifice that is Yahweh's House, as it rises in the Glory and Majesty of Christ.

Israel is both a natural and spiritual entity, formed and fashioned by God the Father as a vessel for the coming of His Son to Earth—"*...a body You have prepared for Me... I have come to do Your will O God*" (Heb. 10:5-7). The Body in which Jesus chose to tabernacle with mankind, fashioned by the Father, over two thousand years for His first coming, is Israel, "*...the Word was made flesh (Jewish flesh) and dwelt (to tabernacle) among us*" (John 1.14).

However, God's work of building His temple has continued over another two thousand years through both Jewish and Gentile people; it will continue to rise in majesty and Glory to meet the King of kings and LORD of lords at His return in Glory.

The Blueprint is a feeble and humble attempt to portray the unsearchable counsels of the Almighty God of Heaven and earth, in His sublime, transcendent, profound and unfathomable work to create and fashion a place of abode for Himself for all eternity.

The Blueprint – Introduction

Most Holy God, Creator of Heaven and Earth,

I come before you in Your great loving kindness and mercy,

To ask that You would graciously open the eyes, the ears and

The understanding of the reader of this work.

Lord, remove any veil that prevents them from seeing Your glorious and

Transcendent plan of redemption, as You have unfolded it over the centuries.

Lord, I plead the Blood of Jesus over all who read this work, and ask that

You would break the power of all anti-Semitic and religious spirits that would

Seek to hinder Your people from seeing the unveiling of

Your Masterpiece—'The Messiah.'

A New Man

"I will make you a great nation...

and in you all the families of the earth

shall be blessed."

Genesis 3:1-3

The Blueprint – A New Man

"The LORD had said to Abram, "Leave your country,

Your people and your father's household

And go to the land I will show you.

"I will make you into a great nation and I will bless you;

I will make your name great, and you will be a blessing.

I will bless those who bless you,

And whoever curses you I will curse;

And all peoples on earth will be blessed through you…"

Genesis 12:1-3

The Blueprint – A New Man

A New Beginning in a New Land

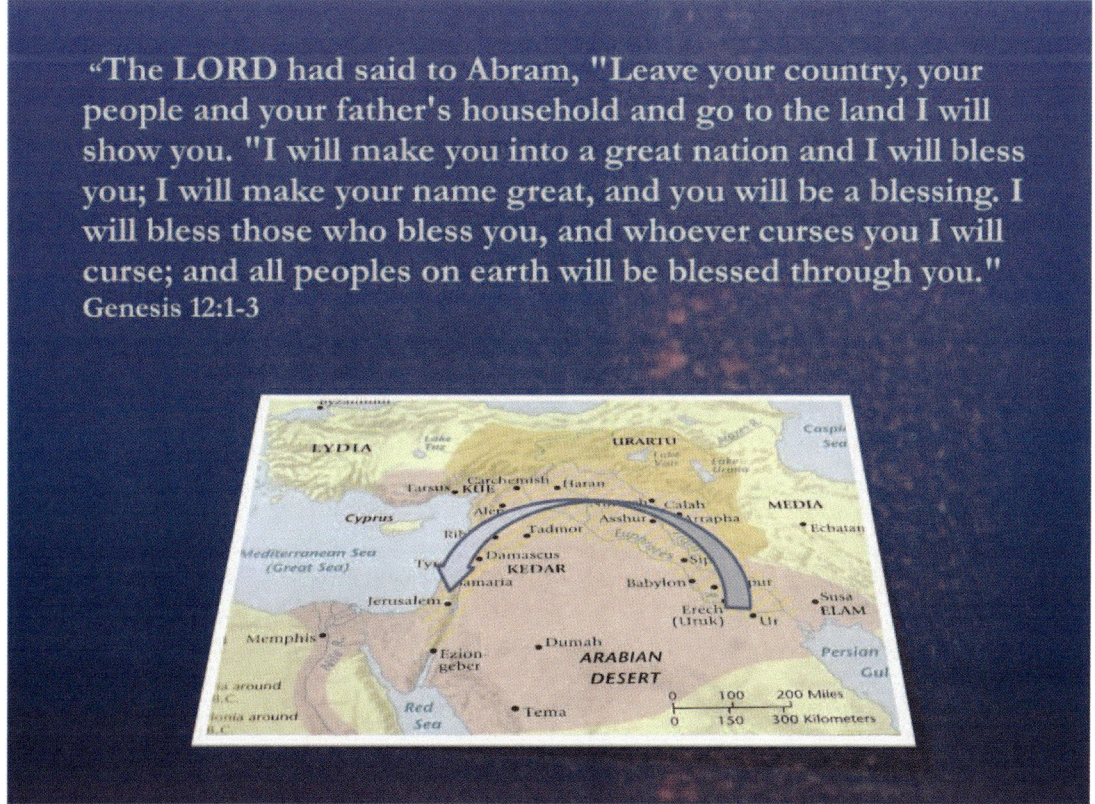

The darkest day in the history of humanity was the day the first created man plunged the world into sin and death. The Earth became corrupted, unclean and defiled in its descent into darkness, giving birth to the spiritual kingdom of Satan the Bible refers to as Babylon. Out of this region, from the land of the Chaldeans, God called out *another man*. His name was Abraham.

The Blueprint – A New Man

"Get out of your country from your family, and from your father's house, to a land that I will show you." Genesis 12:1

The Father's plan for the redemption of the human race began when He chose Abraham as the vessel from whom the prototype of a New Man would be fashioned and formed in the image of His Son. God directed Abraham to leave Ur in the region of Babylon—symbolic of the kingdom of darkness and the fallen world, and go to a new Land that He would show him. Genesis chapter 12:4 reveals Abraham's heart, in that he *"...departed as the LORD had spoken to him."*

"By faith Abraham, when called to go to a place he would later receive as his inheritance, obeyed and went, even though he did not know where he was going. By faith he made his home in the promised land like a stranger in a foreign country; he lived in tents, as did Isaac and Jacob, who were heirs with him of the same promise. For he was looking forward to the city with foundations, whose architect and builder is God." Hebrews 11:8-10

As Babylon, the land of darkness bears the image of Satan, this New Land would bear the image of God—Jesus Christ. Jesus, who is the express image of the Father, is this Land that *"drinks water from heaven"*—the face on the Potter's wheel where the Father's hand would work to shape His New Man and His New Creation called the Heavenly Jerusalem.

In obedience to the LORD, Abraham left the land of darkness in pursuit of God and the land of his destiny. This New Land, chosen by God and separated unto Him for His eternal purposes, therefore became Holy, and is known to this day as the *Holy Land*—the Promised Land of God.

The Blueprint – A New Man

The Promised Land – A New Man in the New Land

In the New Land, God began His magnificent work of fashioning a New Man and transforming him into a Spiritual being conformed to His image. The Master Potter intentioned that Israel be the clay from which He would mold and form this New Man in His Image—a Man in whom the fullness of God would be able to reside. Here *within the boundaries of this land* God chose to work to birth a New Creation, *a New Man* and a New Kingdom characterized by the Light of God.

Israel was God's chosen wineskin prepared as a Body to Host the very Life substance of the Living God, revealed to humanity through Jesus Christ, *"Therefore, when Christ came into the world, he said: "Sacrifice and offering you did not desire, but a body you prepared for me..." (Hebrews 10:5).*

Jesus—the Son of God and the Son of Man was sent to the New Land by the Father, to become the prototype for the New Man. Jesus, the Son of God and very God, humbled Himself to be born in this Land as a Man. He became the fulfillment of all the promises of God to humanity.

Jesus became the second Adam and the First Fruit of a company as numerous as the stars of heaven—sons and daughters with whom He could commune and have fellowship; a corporate vessel that would one day become united with Him in a holy union of Mind, Heart and Spirit.

> *"For as in Adam all die, even so in Christ all shall be made alive." 1Corinthians 15:22*

> *"And so it is written, "The first man Adam became a living being." The last Adam became a life-giving spirit. However, the spiritual is not first, but the natural, and afterward the spiritual. The first man was of the earth, made of dust; the second Man is the Lord from heaven." 1 Corinthians 15:45-47*

Because of the Lord's sacrifice and through His determination and power, a New Man would emerge conformed to His likeness and fashioned to become the dwelling place and habitation of Almighty God—Yahweh's House.

Jerusalem—God Establishes His Throne in the New Land

God has Purposed that the work to restore humanity to the Father's embrace would be accomplished through the nation of Israel and her Seed—Jesus Christ, that through Him, all the families of the earth would be blessed. According to Ezekiel chapter 43:7, God chose Jerusalem as the place where His feet would be positioned and His Throne permanently established.

The Blueprint – A New Man

"For the LORD has chosen Jerusalem; He has desired it for His home. "This is My resting place forever," He said. I will live here, for this is the home I desired. I will bless this city and make it prosperous…" Psalm 132:13-14 NLT

God's plan of redemption was put in motion when in the New Land He set Jerusalem in the midst of nations whose destiny would be determined by their obedience to God, and their relationship to His Land—Israel. Deuteronomy chapter 32:8 states: *"When the Most High divided their inheritance to the nations, when He separated the sons of Adam, He set the boundaries of the peoples according to the number of the children of Israel."*

God decreed Jerusalem to be the Capital of the Promised Land and the centre for all His Kingdom's administrations in the earth—He states in Ezekiel chapter 5:5 'This *is Jerusalem; I have set her in the midst of the nations and the countries all around her."* He declares in Isaiah chapter 2:3, *"The law will go out from Zion, the word of the LORD from Jerusalem."*

Jesus is the King of the Kingdom of God, the Seat of whose Throne is Jerusalem. God established Jerusalem and the land of Israel as the central factor, relative to the whole counsel of God that is inherent in the plan of God for the redemption of humanity, and the restoration of all things to His original intentions.

The Heavenly Jerusalem is the completion of the House begun on the fertile soil of Jacob's life, and whose construction has been taking place over the span of His-story. The Heavenly Jerusalem is the revelation of the Son of God in the fullness of union with mankind. Its gates are constructed in the lives of the twelve tribes of Israel and its walls are built on the foundation of the twelve apostles

The Foundation Stone

"Behold, I lay in Zion a Stone for a foundation…"

Isaiah 28:16

"And they drank of that spiritual Rock that followed them and that Rock was Christ."

1 Corinthians 10:4

"Thus says the LORD: "Heaven is My throne, And earth is My footstool. Where is the house that you will build Me? And where is the place of My rest?"

Isaiah 66:1

"Unless the LORD builds the house,

They labor in vain who build it…"

Psalm 127:1

The Blueprint – The Foundation

The Father lays the Foundation Stone of His Temple

Yahweh Will Provide The Sacrifice!

"Do not lay a hand on the boy," he said. "Do not do anything to him. Now I know that you fear God, because you have not withheld from me your son, your only son." Abraham looked up and there in a thicket he saw a ram caught by its horns. He went over and took the ram and sacrificed it as a burnt offering instead of his son. So Abraham called that place The LORD Will Provide."
Genesis 22:12-14

"Behold I lay in Zion a stone for a *foundation...*" Is. 28:16

Is. 28:16, Gen.35:14-15, Ex. 24:12, 28:10, 1 Ki. 6:7, 1Cor. 10-4

FOUNDATION STONE
The Lamb that was slain from the foundation of the earth

Passover Sacrifice is instituted

In Abraham, the Father found a man in whom He could proceed with His awe-inspiring work of fashioning a New Man through whom He would complete His plans and purposes on earth. God chose Abraham's seed through Isaac then Jacob, to bring forth the Man Christ Jesus, through whom the families of the earth would be blessed, fulfilling the prophecy that Abraham would become the father of many nations.

The Blueprint – The Foundation

Abraham passed the test when in faith and obedience he was willing to offer Isaac his only son with Sarah, as a sacrifice unto God. However, God did not require Abraham's sacrifice—the Father Himself lays the foundation Stone of His Temple; He had the sacrifice already prepared, a ram representing *His* only Son Jesus, the Lamb slain from the foundation of the earth (Rev. 13:8).

Abraham's obedience released God to lay this stone—the sacrifice of an only son—as the foundation stone of His Temple. The Father laid this stone in the soil of Jerusalem, that is the place of His heart and the Seat of His Throne. This site became the future site of the Sacrifice on the Cross of the Father's only begotten Son, Jesus.

Abraham's act of obedience foreshadowed the Passover Feast, becoming the groundbreaking ceremony and commemoration for the laying of the Foundation Stone of Christ for the Temple of God.

This Stone is the Rock of Christ from which Israel drank on their journey in the wilderness, as declared in 1Corinthians 10:4:

> *"...for they drank of that spiritual Rock that followed them, and that Rock was Christ."*

Israel is Established in the New Land as a Nation

> "You brought a vine out of Egypt; you drove out the nations and planted it. You cleared the ground for it, and it took root and filled the land. The mountains were covered with its shade, the mighty cedars with its branches. It sent out its boughs to the Sea, its shoots as far as the River." Psalm 80:8-11
>
> "When Israel was a child, I loved him, and out of Egypt I called my son." Hosea 11:1

ISRAEL Cultivated olive tree Rom. 11:24

Israel

"Behold I lay *in Zion* a stone for a *foundation...*"

ISAAC
FOUNDATION STONE
ABRAHAM

Feast of Firstfruits
Feast of Unleavened Bread
Passover Feast

> "Then say to Pharaoh, 'This is what the LORD says: Israel is my firstborn son.'" Exodus 4:22

After 400 years of slavery in Egypt, God brought His chosen people out with a mighty hand, and with signs and great wonders, fulfilling the prophecy in Hosea 11:1 that, out of Egypt God called forth *His son Israel*.

God instituted the Passover Feast, founded on the sacrifice of a perfect lamb, when Israel left the land of slavery to life in the Presence of Almighty God. God declares to the world in Deuteronomy chapter 4:34, *"Has any other god dared to take a nation for himself out of another nation by means of trials, miraculous signs, wonders, war, a strong hand, a powerful arm and terrifying acts?" (NIV)*

Through Moses, this terrifying God introduced Himself to a people group for the very first time in history. He claimed them as His own, gave them righteous laws to live by, chose to embrace them in arms of love and taught them the protocol of ministering to, and abiding in the Presence of a Holy and Awesome God.

After forty years in the wilderness learning His ways and being refined in the Fire of His Presence, God then replanted Israel in the Holy Land. He established Jerusalem as the place of His Throne, the site where the foundation stone was first laid through Abraham's offering of Isaac. This site would become the future site where the Temple of God would be established and where Jesus the Lamb of God would be sacrificed.

Yahweh's Temple began to rise as He fashions Israel into the vessel through whom He chose to work to bring salvation to the nations of the earth. Jesus declared in John 4:22 that, *"salvation is of the Jews."*

The Blueprint — The Foundation

The Passover Lamb is Sacrificed

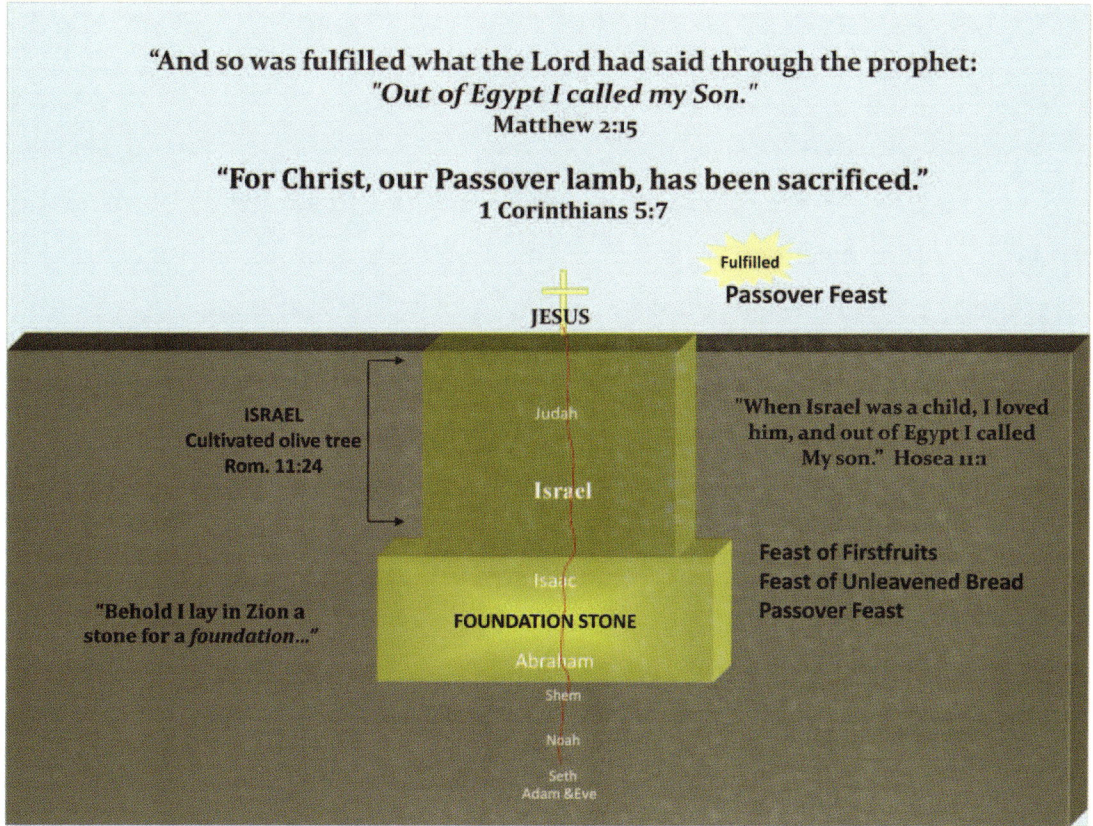

Jesus opened the way for Israel and all humanity to be saved through His obedience to go to the Cross and shed His Blood as the atonement for our sins. The day Jeshua—God's chosen Lamb was sacrificed on the Cross, God's Passover Feast was fulfilled.

> "...He was led as a lamb to the slaughter, and as a sheep before its shearers is silent, so He opened not His mouth." Isaiah 53:7

The Blueprint – The Foundation

The Feasts of the Lord were established by God as *His Feasts*. The celebration of each Feast was His prophetic declaration to Israel and to the world, of key facets of His work to build Himself a House in man individually and corporately.

The multifaceted wisdom of God, the purposes of God, the beginning, the process and the completion, all summed up in Christ, were prophetically declared, and consequently called forth into reality, in the mystery of the ritual and ordinances, practiced year after year, in these seven feasts.

The fulfillment of each Feast marked the completion of a significant phase in the construction of the Temple of God. In Israel's celebration of the Feasts, God, the Alpha and the Omega, was revealing the end from the very beginning. Within these seven feasts, the eternal counsels of God are revealed, and His plan in man and the earth are made complete.

From the very beginning, and throughout history God separated a line unto Himself through whom the Messiah—the Savior of the world, would be born. From Adam's son Seth to Shem, through Israel to the kings of Judah, God preserved a bloodline through whom *the Lion of the tribe of Judah* would be brought forth—the Son of God—the Messiah.

Jesus fulfilled all the prophecies of the Messiah's first coming; He was born in Bethlehem of a virgin, a son of David, from the tribe of Judah. He was the Lamb of God slain for the salvation of humanity; He was the Son of God and the Son of Man, and would be accepted by the Gentiles (Mic.5:1, Is.7:14, Is.53, Is.11:10, Am. 9:12, Ps.2:7).

"Ya'akov was the father of Yosef, the husband of Miryam, from whom was born Yeshua that was called the Messiah." Mattityahu 1:16 JNT

"For to us a child is born, to us a son is given, and the government will be on his shoulders. And he will be called Wonderful Counselor, Mighty God, Everlasting Father, Prince of Peace." Isaiah 9:6

Israel was the body fashioned and prepared to birth the King of Kings at His first coming; When He returns it will be once again through the Beautiful gate of Israel. Hebrew 10:5 states:

"Therefore, when He came into the world, He said: "SACRIFICE AND OFFERING YOU DID NOT DESIRE, BUT A BODY YOU HAVE PREPARED FOR ME."

When Jesus returns, all prophecies of the Messiah will be fulfilled and completed in Him. The eyes of Israel will be opened and they will see their Son and their Messiah.

"On that day I will set out to destroy all the nations that attack Jerusalem. And I will pour out on the house of David and the inhabitants of Jerusalem a spirit of grace and supplication. They will look on me, the one they have pierced, and they will mourn for him as one mourns for an only child, and grieve bitterly for him as one grieves for a firstborn son." Zechariah 12:10 NIV

Jesus is returning to the home where He was born, to the land where He once lived and walked with His friends, and His natural family for thirty-three years. Jesus is going home!

The Blueprint – The Foundation

"And in that day His feet will stand on the Mount of Olives, which faces Jerusalem on the east. And the Mount of Olives shall be split in two, from east to west, making a very large valley; half of the mountain shall move toward the north and half of it toward the south." Zechariah 14:4

The Cornerstone

"The stone which the builders rejected has become

the chief *cornerstone.*"

Psalm. 118:22

"...and that day about three thousand souls

were added to them.

And they continued steadfastly in the apostles' doctrine

And fellowship, in the breaking of bread,

and in prayers."

Acts 2:41

"Your dead shall live; *together with* my dead

Body they shall arise. Awake and sing,

you who dwell in dust;

For your dew *is like* the dew of herbs, and

The earth shall cast out the dead."

Isaiah 26:19

The Blueprint— The Cornerstone

The Superstructure

After Jesus was crucified, and prior to His resurrection, He descended into the depths where He preached to the spirits in prison and extended salvation to the captives (Ephes. 4:8-10 and 1 Pet. 3: 19-20). In His resurrection many of these captives were raised with Him, some of whom were seen by many as Matthew 27:52 states: *"...and the graves were opened; and many bodies of the saints who had fallen asleep were raised and coming out of the graves after His resurrection, they went into the holy city and*

The Blueprint— The Cornerstone

appeared to many." Ephesians 4: 8 teaches that Jesus led these captives in His train as He ascended to the Throne, this Scripture quoted from Psalm 68: 18, goes on to say *'that He might fill all things.'* The Greek word translated as fill, is the word *pleroo*, which means *to complete or to cram full to completion.*

After the crucifixion, Jesus descended to the foundation of His Temple taking hold of Israel past. He then went further pulling in Adam, Eve, Noah, Shem and all the righteous saints—extending the gift of protection to His natural bloodline through the covering of His Blood. He then ascended to the highest place, the Throne of God, in order for the Holy Spirit to be poured out on Israel living at the time. Through Israel, the Holy Spirit was then poured out on the nations of the world, to gather all the chosen of God into the Ark that is 'The Christ,' to cram full to completion His Body—*the Israel of God.*

> *"For I do not desire, brethren, that you should be ignorant of this mystery, lest you should be wise in your own opinion, that blindness in part has happened to Israel until the fullness of the Gentiles has come in."* Romans 11:25

The Cross reaches out in every direction, the past—the righteous of the past, who lived before the Cross, the present and the future—those who have accepted the lordship of Jesus Christ in their lives; all united in the Father's Love through the mercy of the Cross of Calvary

> *"For God so loved the world that he gave his one and only Son, that whoever believes in him shall not perish but have eternal life."* John 3:16

The Blueprint— The Cornerstone

Jesus first 'descended' to the soles of His feet, He then 'ascended' to the place of His Throne, thereby giving form to His spiritual Body (Ez. 43:7). In His ascension journey to the Throne Jesus' previous cry, "it is finished" became a living reality; His work to complete His Spiritual Body was finished. His ascension to the Throne became His final act to bring forth something not previously seen—the Body of Christ—God's Holy Temple.

> *"For God did not send his Son into the world to condemn the world, but to save the world through him. Whoever believes in him is not condemned, but whoever does not believe stands condemned already because he has not believed in the name of God's one and only Son." John 3:17-18*

The Blueprint— The Cornerstone

"No, this is what was spoken by the prophet Joel:

"'In the last days, God says, I will pour out my Spirit on all people.

Your sons and daughters will prophesy, your young men will see visions,

Your old men will dream dreams.

Even on my servants, both men and women,

I will pour out my Spirit in those days, and they will prophesy."

Acts 2:16-18 NIV

The Blueprint— The Cornerstone

The Holy Spirit Breathes Life into the Structure

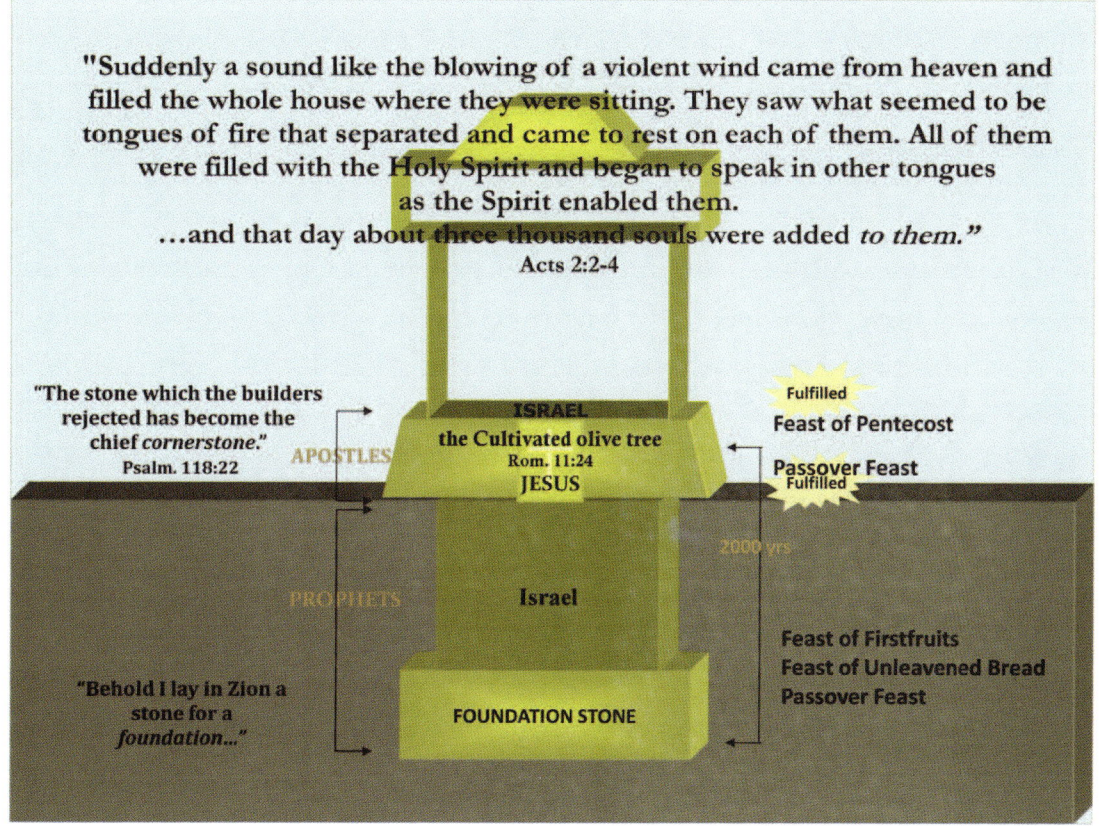

After Jesus ascended to the Father, the way was made clear for the Holy Spirit to be released and poured out on humanity. The sacrifice of the spotless Lamb in whom there was no sin, fulfilled the Passover Feast and released the Holy Spirit to breathe the breath of Life into the Temple, and it became a living breathing entity—a corporate Body indwelt by the Spirit of God.

The Blueprint– The Cornerstone

The Feast of Harvest, also known as Pentecost, was also fulfilled with the outpouring of the Holy Spirit, fifty days after the Sacrifice of the Lamb was offered. Through God's Gift to humanity, of Jesus and the Holy Spirit, He opened a door for a harvest of souls to come into the House of God through the door of Israel.

At Pentecost, the superstructure of the Temple was established in Israel on the foundation of the Jewish apostles and prophets, within the Body of the Jewish King Jesus—*God's* Foundation Stone and now the Chief Cornerstone.

The Olive Tree that is Israel was cultivated by the hands of God from its conception. God began with the offering of Isaac by his father, to the Sacrifice of His Son, Jesus, through to the giving of the Holy Spirit, over a period of approximately two thousand years.

The Superstructure that is the Church or *Ekklesia* of God was established in Israel in the City of Jerusalem, by Jewish apostles, with Jewish congregants. The Greek word Ekklesia, simply means the assembly of God, it is the same word used for the congregation of Israel in the Septuagint—the Greek translation of the Old Testament, the apostles and the early church used.

God's plan of redemption for Israel still stands and His covenant with them, is eternal, as stated repeatedly in His Word:

> *"And so all Israel will be saved, as it is written:* "THE DELIVERER WILL COME OUT OF ZION, AND HE WILL TURN AWAY UNGODLINESS FROM JACOB; FOR THIS IS MY COVENANT WITH THEM, WHEN I TAKE AWAY THEIR SINS." *Romans 11:26-27*

The Blueprint— The Cornerstone

"He remembers His covenant forever, The word which He commanded, for a thousand generations, the covenant which He made with Abraham, and His oath to Isaac, and confirmed it to Jacob for a statute, to Israel as an everlasting covenant." Psalm 105:8-10

"And I will establish My covenant between Me and you and your descendants after you in their generations, for an everlasting covenant, to be God to you and your descendants after you." Genesis 17:7

"On that day I will raise up the tabernacle of David,

Which has fallen down, and repair its damages; I will

Raise up its ruins, and rebuild it as in the days of old;

That they may possess the remnant of Edom,

And all the Gentiles who are called by My name,"

Says the LORD who does this thing."

Amos 9:11-12

The Blueprint— The Cornerstone

The Gentiles are Invited to Enter

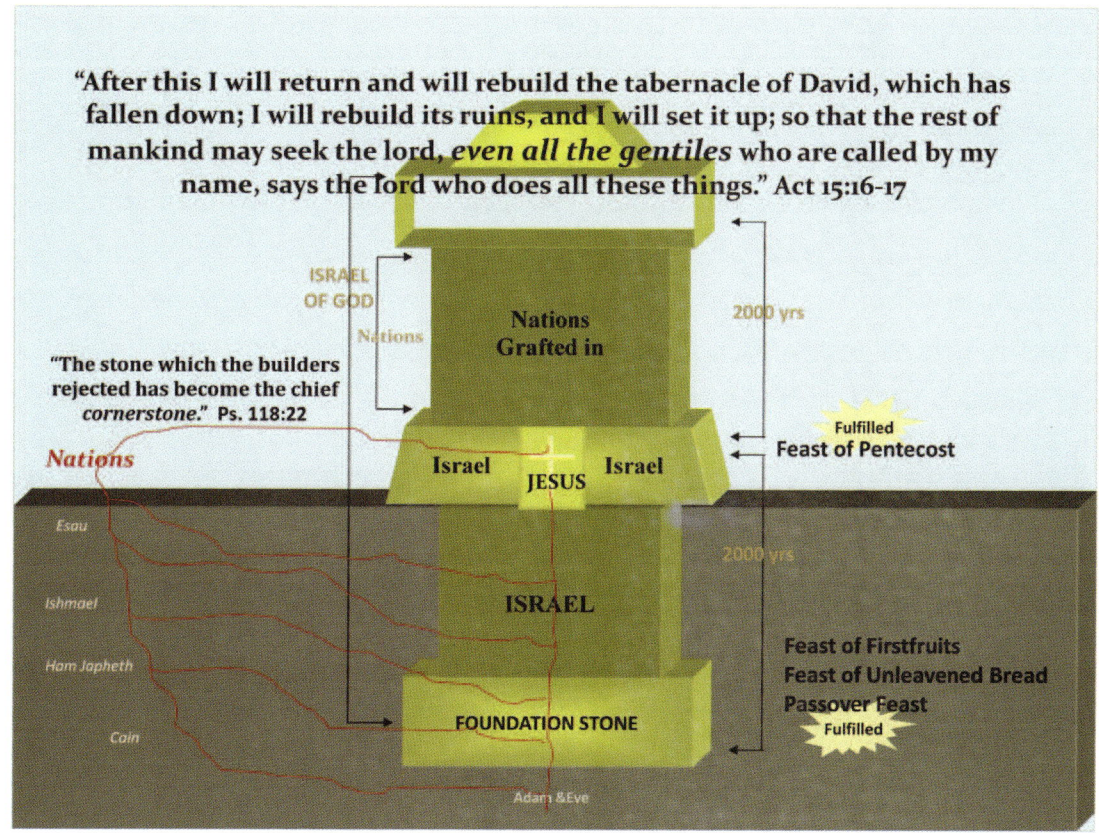

Through the Blood of Jesus, and with the coming of the Holy Spirit, the way was made possible for a Harvest of Gentile souls to be grafted into 'the Israel of God' as prophesied by Joel, *"I will pour out My Spirit on all flesh."* The nations were given the opportunity to draw near to God through the covenants and the promises given to Israel and made available through Jesus—the Son of Israel. At the Jerusalem council that met to discuss the phenomenon of Gentiles receiving salvation in Jesus, James quotes the Word of God spoken through the prophet Amos. Amos prophesied that the Tabernacle of David would one day be rebuilt, and would become a place where all humanity could seek the Lord. Paul further explains this mystery, hidden even to the prophets in Ephesians 2:11-22.

> *"Therefore, remember that formerly you who are Gentiles by birth and called uncircumcised....remember that at that time you were separate from Christ, excluded from citizenship in Israel and foreigners to the covenants of the promise, without hope and without God in the world. But now in Christ Jesus you who once were far away have been brought near through the blood of Christ..." (NIV)*

Paul further states:

> *"Consequently, you are no longer foreigners and aliens, but fellow citizens with God's people and members of God's household, built on the foundation of the apostles and prophets, with Christ Jesus himself as the chief cornerstone. In him the whole building is joined together and rises to become a holy temple in the Lord. And in him you too are being built together to become a dwelling in which God lives by his Spirit." NIV*

God began His restoration of the Tabernacle of David at the Feast of Harvest (Pentecost), with the outpouring of the Holy Spirit in Jerusalem—the City of David. At this Feast, God began the process of gathering in a harvest of souls, first from Israel. God established His Church or *Ekklesia*, on the foundation of the apostles and prophets *in Israel*, in Jesus. Salvation is to the Jew first, and the Glory is to the Jew first according to Romans 1:16:

The Blueprint— The Cornerstone

> *"I am not ashamed of the gospel, because it is the power of God for the salvation of everyone who believes: first for the Jew, then for the Gentile,"* and Romans 2:10: *"...but glory, honor and peace for everyone who does good: first for the Jew, then for the Gentile."*

With the outpouring of the Holy Spirit, the nations, drawn by God's love, began to be gathered into the Temple of God through the door of the Cross—a Cross that was driven into the soil of *Jerusalem*—the Holy land, where the Blood of the Son of God was spilled. In speaking to the nations in Romans chapter 11:17, Paul admonishes Gentiles not to be arrogant, as we are the wild olive shoot grafted in to Israel, God's cultivated olive tree, cultivated in the soil of His love over a period of two thousand years.

> *"If some of the branches have been broken off, and you, though a wild olive shoot, have been grafted in among the others and now share in the nourishing sap from the olive root, do not boast over those branches If you do, consider this: You do not support the root, but the root supports you.*
>
> *You will say then, "Branches were broken off so that I could be grafted in." Granted. But they were broken off because of unbelief, and you stand by faith. Do not be arrogant, but be afraid.*
>
> *For if God did not spare the natural branches, he will not spare you either. Consider therefore the kindness and sternness of God: sternness to those who fell, but kindness to you, provided that you continue in his kindness. Otherwise, you also will be cut off.*
>
> *And if they do not persist in unbelief, they will be grafted in, for God is able to graft them in again. After all, if you were cut out of an olive tree that is*

wild by nature, and contrary to nature were grafted into a cultivated olive tree, how much more readily will these, the natural branches, be grafted into their own olive tree!"

The Headstone

"Not by might, nor by power, but by my spirit,

Saith the LORD of hosts.

Who art thou, O great mountain? Before Zerubbabel

Thou shalt become a plain.

And he shall bring forth the headstone thereof with

shoutings, crying, Grace, grace unto it."

Zechariah 4:6-7 KJV

The Blueprint — The Headstone

"All by itself the soil produces grain—

First the stalk,

Then the head,

Then the full kernel in the head."

Mark 4:28

The Blueprint — The Headstone

The Body grows up to the Head

Yahweh's House is an ongoing work begun by God the Father four thousand years ago on the soil of the life of Abraham, Isaac and Israel. The foundations were established; the superstructure was brought forth at Pentecost, and the foundation of the final phase—*the Headstone*—is now being laid. *'He shall bring forth the headstone with shouts of grace!'* (Zech. 4:7).

The Blueprint – The Headstone

Over the centuries, from the time of Abraham, God worked to build precept on precept, in the measure that His people were able to appropriate these truths and principles. He unveiled revelations of Himself, and established His nature, character, and ways into the structure that was to become His Dwelling place. Through each of the first six Houses of worship, God laid foundational truths of Himself and His ways into the structure and DNA of His Temple.

Through Moses' tabernacle, He laid the foundation of Law thereby establishing order within the community of His people; through David's tabernacle, He laid the foundations of worship, praise and honor; Solomon's Temple revealed the awesome magnificence, Glory and goodness of the Sovereign Lord, and Zerubbabel's temple revealed the wonderful mercy and faithfulness of a loving God.

Herod's Temple, built over forty six years, represented the utter uselessness of flesh, and the futility of man's attempt to build a dwelling for God; this was the temple in question, to which Jesus said, *"destroy this temple and in three days I will rebuild it"* (John 2:19-20). Apart from the wall that still stands today as a reminder of the consequences of abandoning God, this temple was utterly destroyed by the Romans in 70 A.D.

To this present day, God has not allowed the rebuilding of another physical temple, as Jesus, Son of God and very God, came as the fulfillment of the Law and representative of all the fullness of God. The temple of stone became a living breathing entity that is, 'The Christ,' filled with the very Life of God.

The Blueprint – The Headstone

Much of God's Blueprint of the Temple, His Christ, was lost over time especially through the Dark Ages. God is now working to restore all that was lost; saints are now being called to return to build the Headstone—the seventh and last temple or phase, to complete the awesome edifice that is 'The Christ,' whose span touches the very Throne of God.

These six temples have all been stages in the work of God over history to build Himself One Magnificent Temple blueprinted in Christ. The seventh stage and last Temple will be one that is pure and Holy unto the Lord, built without the defilement of flesh and the carnality of division and prejudice. It will be a Temple without spot or wrinkle, as this one will be the one that receives the King in Glory at His Return.

The span of the Temple of God is, the Son of God at the beginning—the foundation and pattern of the Temple; the Son of Man on the Cross at the Crossroads of His-story, drawing into *Agape* love all those who belong to Him by faith, who came before and were to come after; and the Son of God at the end—His Body filled with all the Fullness of the Godhead as He reigns in Glory in union with His Body.

Jesus was at the beginning and He stands victorious in Majesty at the end as *both*, "**the Root *and* the Offspring of David…**" (Rev. 22:16). The Temple of God is Jesus in union with man—Deity in full union with humanity.

The Blueprint – The Headstone

"Instead, speaking the truth in love,

We will in all things grow up into him who is the Head,

That is, Christ.

From him the whole body,

Joined and held together by every supporting ligament,

Grows and builds itself up in love, as each part does its work."

Ephesians 4:15-16

The Blueprint – The Headstone

The Headstone Completed in Christ

We are now living in the times of the restoration of 'all things' as God along with the heavenly hosts work to restore His Temple to the Blueprint it was first founded on. The Headstone, that is the last phase of the building work, is the final covering that completes the Temple. The Headstone will come forth in the power of the Holy Spirit, with Great Grace, as God's work in man reaches its fullness through love.

The Blueprint — The Headstone

"See, the stone I have set in front of Joshua! There are seven eyes on that one stone, and I will engrave an inscription on it,' says the LORD Almighty, 'and I will remove the sin of this land in a single day." Zechariah 3:9

According to Revelation 5:6, the seven eyes represent the seven Spirits of God. The Headstone will characterize the whole counsel of God and will represent the Son of God in fullness. In these last days, God is working to bring the Body of Christ into a Holy Union with His Mind and His Heart, and once again caught up in the momentum of His Will.

God is presently releasing His saints from the captivity and the mindset of religious pride and presumption, to build the Headstone according to the blueprint He ordained His Temple to be built, two thousand years ago. The heavens are opening and the Body is receiving—as at the beginning—a fresh revelation of 'The Christ'—the Ark of God.

God is preparing a chosen Headstone people in these last days to work together to build the Headstone as the covering that will complete His Temple. The whole earth has been awaiting the revelation of these headstone people—'sons of God' who are of the Stature of Christ. These sons, comprised of Jew and Gentile, become *one New Man* in union with Christ and the purposes of Christ.

The New Man will give honor to the work God has accomplished in humanity through Israel, as God restores Israel once again as the Head and not the tail, and restores Jerusalem as the place of His Throne and the Place of the soles of His feet, where He has chosen to dwell forever (Ez. 43:7).

The Blueprint – The Headstone

> *"The hands of Zerubbabel Have laid the foundation of this temple; His hands shall also finish it. Then you will know that the LORD of hosts has sent Me to you. For who has despised the day of small things? For these seven rejoice to see the plumb line in the hand of Zerubbabel. They are the eyes of the LORD, which scan to and fro throughout the whole earth." Zechariah 4:9-10*

The LORD, Yahweh, rejoices when the Plumb Line that is Jesus, the Son of Israel, is placed in the hands of Israel, the fathers who began the building work on the Temple of God, and who will work with the Gentile church to complete it. This is God's word to Israel today:

> *"Yet now be strong, Zerubbabel,' says the LORD; 'and be strong, Joshua, son of Jehozadak, the high priest; and be strong, all you people of the land,' says the LORD, **'and work; for I am with you,'** says the LORD of hosts. 'According to the word that I covenanted with you when you came out of Egypt, so My Spirit remains among you; do not fear!' "For thus says the LORD of hosts: 'Once more (it is a little while) I will shake heaven and earth, the sea and dry land; and I will shake all nations, and they shall come to the Desire of All Nations, and I will fill this temple with glory,' says the LORD of hosts." Haggai 2:4-7*

The Government of God, resting on the shoulders of Jesus—the Son of Israel and the Head of the Body, will be firmly established in the Headstone in the union of Jew and Gentile, in Christ. God the Father has chosen the Israel and the Gentile Christians as vessels through which the Holy anointing oil flows out to touch humanity with His Presence—they are two vessels of oil having one Source, and together they become one in Him.

The Blueprint – The Headstone

"What are these two olive trees—at the right of the lampstand and at its left?" And I further answered and said to him, "What are these two olive branches that drip into the receptacles of the two gold pipes from which the golden oil drains?" Then he answered me and said, "Do you not know what these are?" And I said, "No, my lord." So he said, "These are the two anointed ones, who stand beside the Lord of the whole earth." Zechariah 4:14

We have now arrived at the final page of His-story where we must come together in unity to build and prepare the seventh Temple—*the Most Holy Place*—the Headstone of the superstructure. God is now releasing those who will work with Him to complete this last phase of the building work. These are ones with ears to hear; who are willing and obedient; ready to embrace the Cross to follow Him, ready to lay down all of their 'stuff,' ones who are ready to embrace Israel fully. He is now bringing forth His builders—His apostles, prophets, evangelists, teachers and pastors, to work with Him as at the beginning.

The One New Man

"For in Him we live and move and have our being"

Acts 17:28

The Blueprint – One New Man

"But now in Christ Jesus you who once were far away have

been brought near through the blood of Christ.

For he himself is our peace, who has made the two one and

Has destroyed the barrier, the dividing wall of hostility,

By abolishing in his flesh the law with its commandments

And regulations. His purpose was to create in himself

One new man out of the two, thus making peace,

and in this one body to reconcile both of them to God

through the cross, by which he put to death their hostility.

He came and preached peace to you who were far away

And peace to those who were near.

For through him we both have access to the Father by one Spirit."

Ephesians 2:13-18

The One New Man is Birthed

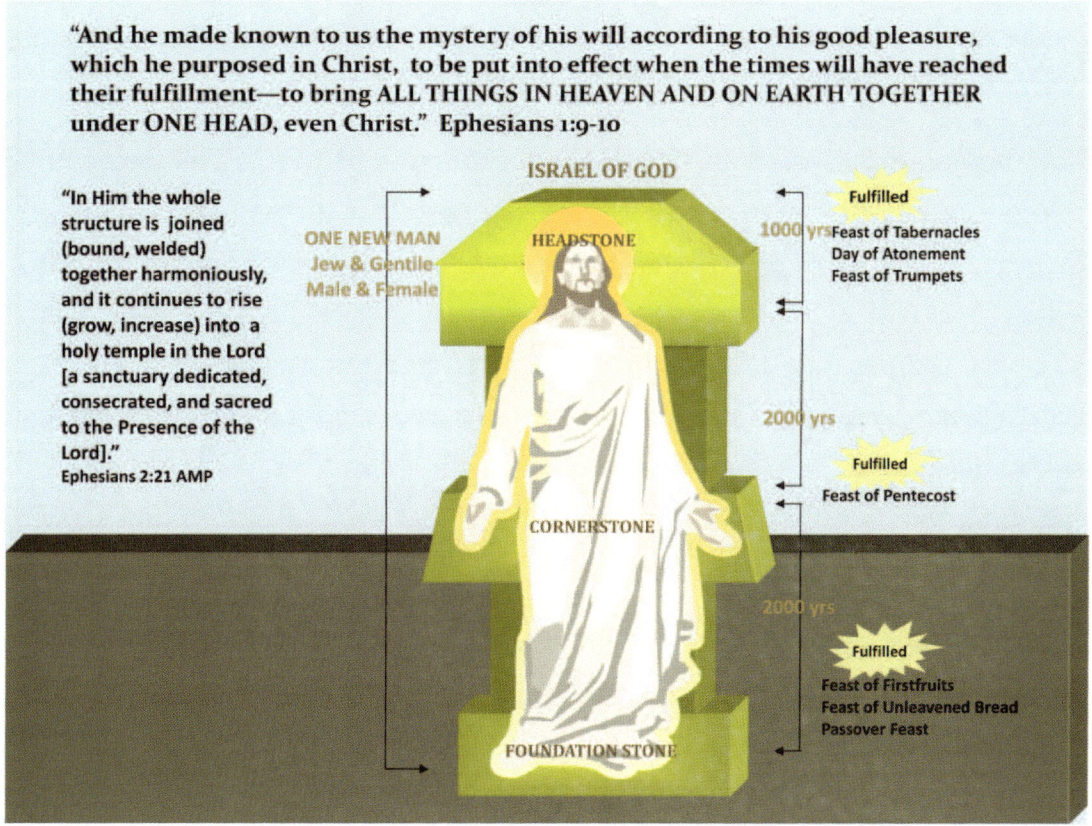

The Headstone will be fully represented through the one New Man of both Jew and Gentile, and male and female; it is fashioned in the crucible of Israel, and will be administered through the five-fold ministry of Jesus. The refining and preparation process continues until all have come, *"to the measure of the stature of the fullness of Christ;"* and have grown up *"... in all things into Him who is the head—Christ."* *(*Eph 4:11-16).

The Blueprint – One New Man

"In Him the whole structure is joined (bound, welded) together harmoniously, and it continues to rise (grow, increase) into a holy temple in the Lord [a sanctuary dedicated, consecrated, and sacred to the presence of the Lord]." Ephesians 2:21 AMP

The Temple of God built on Hebraic roots is a Man. The Headstone represents a mature man of the stature of Christ. It is the union of many built together in Christ, *"For in Him we live and move and have our being."* Jesus Christ is as vast in depth as our forever expanding universe, yet every detail of God's Temple is to be true to Him, nothing is left to chance or to flesh, Romans 11:33 declares, *"O, the depth of the riches both of the wisdom and knowledge of God!"*

Every detail of His first coming—the manner in which He came, the nation and culture He chose to born into, that was the body prepared for Him (Heb. 10:5); the life He lived and walked for thirty three years, the principles that He taught, and His death on the Cross—are all vital parts of the Blueprint of the future habitation of God in corporate Man. If we build *what He built,* He will return to fill it.

When the Tabernacle of Moses and the temple of Solomon were completed, both according to God's specifications, the Glory of God descended and filled these temples. When Ezekiel's temple was completed, at the end of nine chapters of specifications, God's declaration over it was, *'Yahweh Shamah'— the LORD He is there.*

No man can build the Temple of God, as its measure is 'The Christ,' and the Holy Spirit alone has the complete Blueprint. Jesus, Son of God and Son of

The Blueprint — One New Man

Israel is both the Blueprint of the House of God and the Pattern of the New Man God has been fashioning over the centuries.

The measure that the structure we have built, corresponds to the structure He has built, is the measure of the Glory we will appropriate. *God will fill what He builds.*

As we approach the times of the fulfillment of all things, the veil between Heaven and Earth will progressively be removed, as Heaven and Earth unite in the Headstone, under the Headship and government of the King of kings, Jesus Christ.

"The LORD reigns, let the nations tremble;

He sits enthroned between the cherubim,

Let the earth shake.

Great is the LORD in Zion;

He is exalted over all the nations.

Let them praise your great and awesome name—

He is holy."

Psalm 99:1-3

Jesus—the Plumb Line of the Yahweh's House

Faith Marie Baczko

Jesus is the Plumb Line the Father has used to test all measures and standards pertaining to His House. *"A plumb-bob or a plummet is a weight, usually with a pointed tip on the bottom, which is suspended from a string and used as a vertical reference line, or plumb-line"* (Wikipedia). The pointed tip of the plumb line is drawn by gravitational force to locate the center of gravity—the law of gravity therefore governs the behavior of the plumb line.

The Blueprint – One New Man

God uses the Plumb Line of Jesus Christ who is the Word of God incarnate, as the foundation and vertical reference of His temple, as it is built upward and rises in Glory to the Throne of God. Jesus' Life is the gravitational pull that forever works to bring all things into alignment to His Standard.

> *"For God was pleased to have all his fullness dwell in him, and through him to reconcile to himself all things, whether things on earth or things in heaven, by making peace through his blood, shed on the cross." Colossians 1:19-20 NIV*

Those who have disregarded the Standard of Jesus' life when attempting to build God's House, have produced—similar to the leaning Tower of Pisa, a structure that is off centre or distorted, devoid of the beauty and Majesty of Christ. It is impossible for such a structure to be the eternal habitation of the Everlasting God.

The absolutes of the Word of God must be the Plumb Line of the House that He has designed for Himself, as His place of abode. As the structure goes up God carefully ensures that everything pertaining to His House is true to 'Plumb.' In our quest for God's Glory, the means we use to get to the finish line is as important as the destination.

The absolutes of Christ and God's Word are not intended to limit, but rather to release the freedom found in the resurrection Life of Christ. Our God is a Holy God and He is known in Scripture as the God of patience; throughout history, as man has veered in the wrong direction, away from the Plumb Line, God has continually worked to bring him back to the magnificence of Christ in all His attributes, His features and His DNA.

The Blueprint – One New Man

> *"Thus He showed me: Behold, the Lord stood on a wall made with a plumb line, with a plumb line in His hand. And the LORD said to me, "Amos, what do you see?" And I said, "A plumb line." Then the Lord said: "Behold, I am setting a plumb line In the midst of My people Israel; I will not pass by them anymore." Amos 7:7*

The House that Jesus returns to will be the House that He has designed, built from the Blueprint ordained by the Father and constructed with the substance of Sacrificial Love.

As we approach the times of the fulfillment of all things, the veil between heaven and earth will progressively be removed, as heaven and earth unite in the headstone, under the Headship and government of the King of kings, Jesus Christ.

> *"And he made known to us the mystery of his will according to his good pleasure, which he purposed in Christ, to be put into effect when the times will have reached their fulfilment—to bring ALL THINGS IN HEAVEN AND ON EARTH TOGETHER under ONE HEAD, even Christ." Ephesians 1:9-10 NIV*

"Blessed be the LORD out of Zion,

Who dwells in Jerusalem!

Praise the LORD!"

Psalm 135:21

The Government of God is Established in Zion

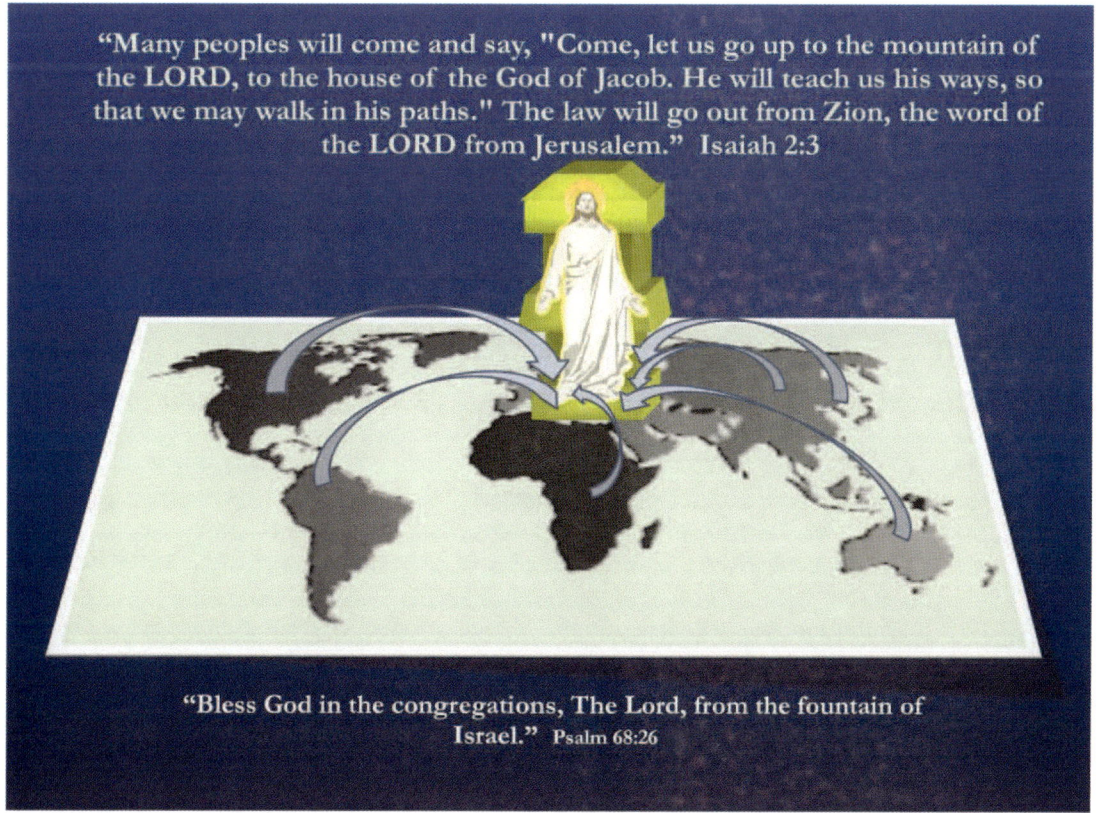

Jesus will one day return to planet, earth and many are being called as servants who will work with the Lord to prepare His way. We do not know the date that He will return, but whatever amount of time that He has given us, it is exactly the amount of time needed to gather in the Harvest, and to make ready the Body of Christ. The final procession of the King into His Sanctuary, as He takes His place on the Throne of God established in Israel, is revealed in Psalm 68:24-35:

The Blueprint – One New Man

*"Your procession has come into view, O God, the procession of my God and King into the sanctuary. In front are the singers, after them the musicians; with them are the maidens playing tambourines. Praise God in the great congregation; praise the LORD in the **assembly of Israel**. There is the little tribe of Benjamin, leading them, there the great throng of Judah's princes, and there the princes of Zebulun and of Naphtali. Summon your power, O God; show us your strength, O God, as you have done before.*

Because of your temple at Jerusalem, kings will bring you gifts. Envoys will come from Egypt; Cush will submit herself to God.

Sing to God, O kingdoms of the earth, sing praise to the Lord, Selah to him who rides the ancient skies above, who thunders with mighty voice.

Proclaim the power of God, whose majesty is over Israel, whose power is in the skies.

You are awesome, O God, in your sanctuary; the God of Israel gives power and strength to his people. Praise be to God!" (NIV)

The Hebrew word for assembly in verse 26 is *maqor*, which means, *something dug, a source of water, tears or blood, a fountain.* We are admonished to praise the Lord from the assembly or fountain of Israel, the place from where the Blood of Jesus flowed and the Father's tears were shed for His Son and for humanity. The headwaters of the River of God that began to flow on the Day of Pentecost, is set in Israel. Israel will once again be restored to her place of honor:

"Many peoples will come and say, come, let us go up to the mountain of the LORD, to the house of the God of Jacob. He will teach us his ways, so that

we may walk in his paths. The law will go out from Zion, the word of the LORD from Jerusalem" Isaiah 2:3.

Jesus—the Messiah, will one day return to Jerusalem to fulfill all prophecies and complete God's work. His feet will stand on the Mount of Olives as the Word of God declares (Zech. 14:4), and His Government of the nations will be centered and established in Jerusalem (Is.2:3); of the increase of His government there shall be no end (Is. 9:7). Princes will reign with Him in righteousness, and with Him, will rule the nations with a rod of iron (Rev. 2:27, 12:5).

"Behold, a king will reign in righteousness, And princes will rule with justice. A man will be as a hiding place from the wind, and a cover from the tempest, As rivers of water in a dry place, as the shadow of a great rock in a weary land." Isaiah32:1-2

The Blueprint – One New Man

"I have installed my King on Zion, my holy hill."

I will proclaim the decree of the LORD: He said to me,

"You are my Son; today I have become your Father.

Ask of me, and I will make the nations your inheritance,

The ends of the earth your possession.

You will rule them with an iron scepter;

You will dash them to pieces like pottery."

Therefore, you kings, be wise; be warned, you rulers of the earth

Serve the LORD with fear and rejoice with trembling.

Kiss the Son, lest he be angry and you be destroyed in your way,

For his wrath can flare up in a moment.

Blessed are all who take refuge in him."

Psalm 2:6-12 NIV

The Government Shall be upon His Shoulders

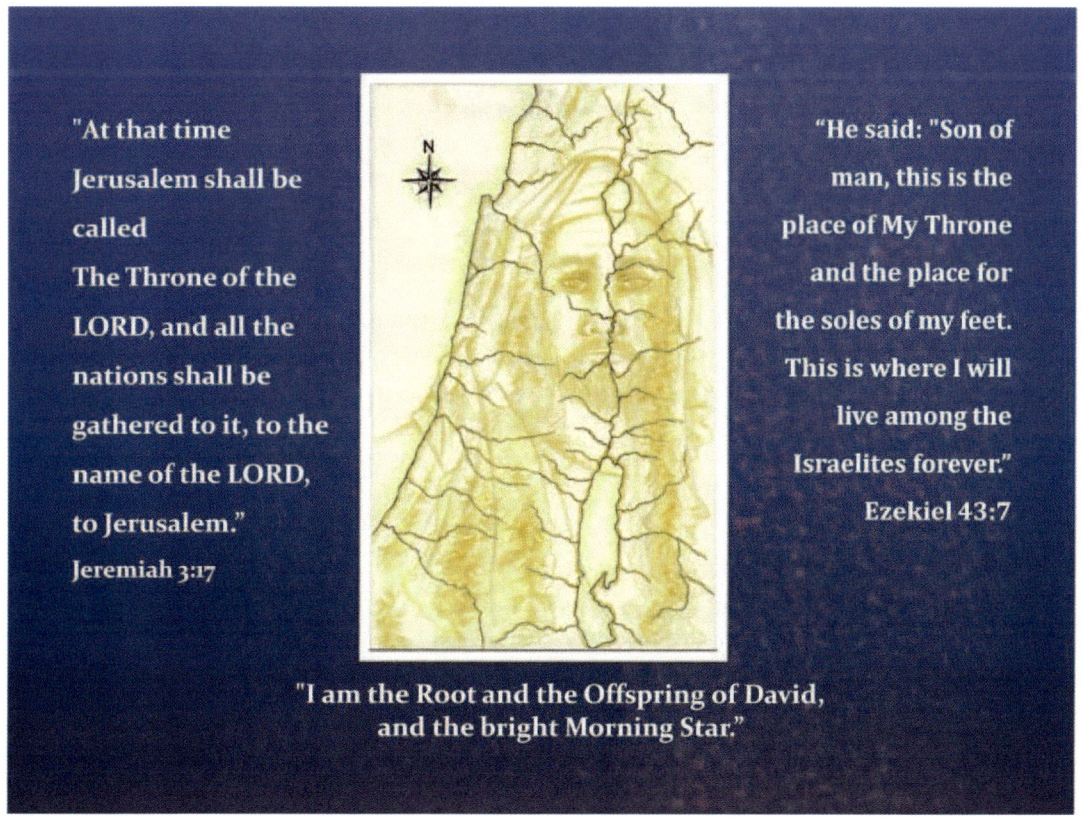

The whole issue of Israel and Jerusalem can be reduced to one theme, and that is one of Government. God has chosen Jerusalem as the one location, set in the center of the nations, from where He would establish His Government and administrate His Kingdom. From the very beginning, this has been contested by the kingdom of darkness through the kingdoms of this world. The battle over who will have dominion of the earth, presently raging in the spiritual realm and continually erupting in the natural realm, is centered in Israel. Israel, the key to the government and rule of the Kingdom of God on earth will remain the center of the battle until the King returns.

> *"Of the increase of his government and peace there will be no end. He will reign on David's throne and over his kingdom, establishing and upholding it with justice and righteousness from that time on and forever. The zeal of the LORD Almighty will accomplish this." Isaiah 9:7 (NIV)*

> *"He will be great and will be called the Son of the Most High. The Lord God will give him the throne of his father David, and he will reign over the house of Jacob forever; his kingdom will never end." Luke 1:33 (NIV)*

> *"At that time Jerusalem shall be called The Throne of the LORD, and all the nations shall be gathered to it, to the name of the LORD, to Jerusalem." Jeremiah 3:17 (NIV)*

> *"For the LORD has chosen Zion; He has desired it for His dwelling place: "This is My resting place forever; Here I will dwell, for I have desired it." Psalm 132:13-14 (NIV)*

When the Government of God is established in Jerusalem through His King Jesus Christ, only then will the nations of the earth have peace! At the return of Jesus to Zion, all the nations of the earth will be required to send a delegation to Jerusalem to worship the King and celebrate the Feast of Tabernacles; if they do not they will experience plagues and will not have rain (Zech. 14:16-19). This prophecy has begun to be fulfilled in measure, as thousands of saints from the nations of the world go up every year to worship the Lord at this Feast.

The Bride of Christ

"...Let the bridegroom go out from His chamber,

And the bride from her dressing room."

Joel 2:16

"Let us rejoice and be glad and give him glory!

For the wedding of the Lamb has come,

and his bride has made herself ready."

Revelation 19:7 NIV

The Blueprint – The Bride of Christ

The Bride is Presented

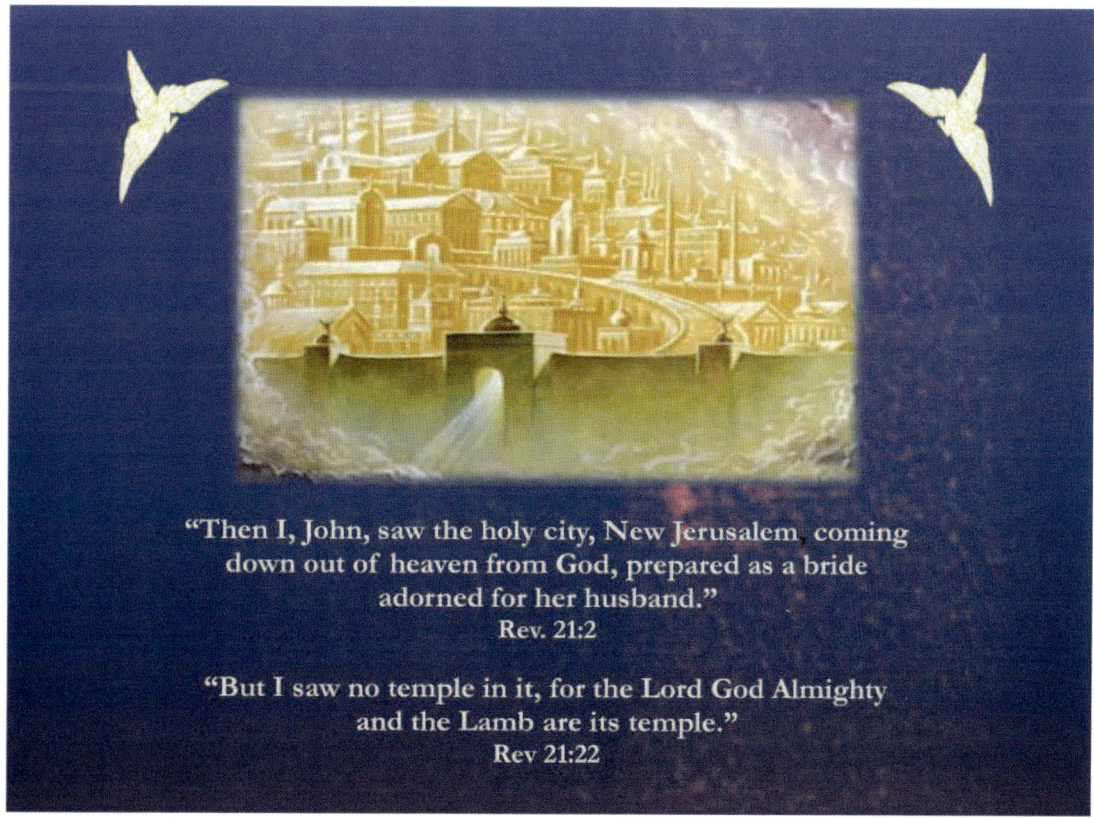

The Majestic unveiling of God's masterpiece—His Bride, that is the Union of God and man, is represented in the Holy City—the New Jerusalem, seen coming down out of Heaven prepared for her Bridegroom. Jerusalem is representative of God's heart, whenever our hearts are united with God's heart in love, through the Holy Spirit, God's Presence and heart for Jerusalem is manifested. Jerusalem is the Bride of Christ, and is one with the Father and the Holy Spirit. God says to Jerusalem in Ezekiel, 16:6-8:

The Blueprint – The Bride of Christ

"And when I passed by you and saw you struggling in your own blood, I said to you in your blood, 'Live!' Yes, I said to you in your blood, 'Live!' ... I made you thrive like a plant in the field; and you grew, matured, and became very beautiful. Your breasts were formed, your hair grew, but you were naked and bare. "When I passed by you again and looked upon you, indeed your time was the time of love; so I spread My wing over you and covered your nakedness. Yes, I swore an oath to you and entered into a covenant with you, and you became Mine," says the Lord GOD.

In the Old Testament, Israel and Jerusalem are referred to as God's Bride many times indirectly and seven times directly. In the great body of Church doctrine, laid down in the New Testament by Paul and other apostles, the word 'bride' is never mentioned directly, and only once indirectly.

In the Gospels, the word 'bride' is mentioned once in John 3:9 where John refers to Jesus as the Bridegroom and Israel as His Bride; it is mentioned three times in the book of Revelations at the completion of God's work in mankind, summed up in Christ, in the Holy City of Jerusalem.

Every word and detail in the Bible included or excluded is intentional by God, and is with purpose. God's intention for deliberately excluding the word bride from the body of doctrine in the epistles, may be that Gentiles, who, throughout the history of the Church have been attempting to replace themselves with Israel, might have been given the occasion to do so. The Gentile Church is the Bride of Christ only as it has been grafted into the Bride—the Israel of God. God says of Jerusalem in Isaiah 62:5-7:

The Blueprint – The Bride of Christ

> *"As a young man marries a maiden, so will your sons marry you; as a bridegroom rejoices over his bride, so will your God rejoice over you. I have posted watchmen on your walls, O Jerusalem; they will never be silent day or night. You who call on the LORD, give yourselves no rest, and give him no rest till he establishes Jerusalem and makes her the praise of the earth." (NIV)*

The Hebrew word for bride is *kallah,* which means, a *bride – as if perfect*, it is from the root word *kalah* meaning, *to complete and make perfect*. In the times of the summing up of all things in Christ, God will bring Jerusalem, that is the Israel of God—*the one new man of Jew and Gentile*—to completion and perfection, to be unveiled as the most beautiful Bride for His Glory.

> *"The royal daughter is all glorious within the palace; her clothing is woven with gold. She shall be brought to the King in robes of many colors; the virgins, her companions who follow her, shall be brought to You. With gladness and rejoicing they shall be brought; they shall enter the King's palace." Psalm 45:13-15*

Jesus is both the Root and the Offspring of Israel, He is the Alpha and the Omega; He is the beginning and the completion of the Israel of God.

> *"...I am the Root and the Offspring of David, and the bright Morning Star." Revelation 22:16 (NIV)*

In the Glorious City of Jerusalem, the structure that was the Temple of God, so meticulously prepared over four thousand years from the time of Abraham to the return of Christ, is consumed in the Glory, and has become a Bride. In eternity, the Temple ceases to exist, for the LORD God Almighty and the Lamb are the Temple.

"But I saw no temple in it, for the Lord God Almighty and the Lamb are its temple. The city had no need of the sun or of the moon to shine in it, for the glory of God illuminated it. The Lamb is its light." Revelation 21:22-23

"Come, I will show you the bride, the wife of the Lamb."

And he carried me away in the Spirit to a mountain great and high, and showed me the Holy City, Jerusalem, coming down out of heaven from God.

It shone with the glory of God, and its brilliance was like that of a very precious jewel, like a jasper, clear as crystal.

It had a great, high wall with twelve gates, and with twelve angels at the gates.

On the gates were written the names of the twelve tribes of Israel."

The Blueprint – The Bride of Christ

Israel honored in Eternity

God's intent for both Jews and Gentiles, is contained in His master plan, revealed in Paul's letter to the Romans, chapter 11:29-33 states:

"For as you were once disobedient to God, yet have now obtained mercy through their disobedience, even so these also have now been disobedient, that through the mercy shown you they also may obtain mercy. For God has committed them all to disobedience, that He might have mercy on all.

The Blueprint – The Bride of Christ

> *Oh the depth of the riches both of the wisdom and knowledge of God! How unsearchable are His judgments and His ways past finding out!"*

After a thousand years of rule on earth, all the carnality and iniquity of the Gentile church and Israel will be consumed in the fire of God's love (1Cor. 3:15). Everything that could have been shaken, would have been shaken, all that remains of the Edifice of God is the Foundation Stone, the Cornerstone and the Headstone that is 'THE CHRIST!'

The City of God that Abraham longed for is built on the twelve foundations of the apostles who were all Israelites; and the twelve gates leading into the City were honored with the names of the twelve tribes of Israel. God has chosen to give honor to Israel throughout eternity as the little gate through which all who humbled themselves would enter the Holy City.

> *"Also she had a great and high wall with twelve gates, and twelve angels at the gates, and names written on them, which are the names of the twelve tribes of the children of Israel: three gates on the east, three gates on the north, three gates on the south, and three gates on the west." Revelation 21:12-13*

> *"The twelve gates were twelve pearls: each individual gate was of one pearl." Revelation 21:21*

God's Everlasting Covenant with Israel

And I will make an EVERLASTING COVENANT with them, that I will not turn away from doing them good; but I will put my fear in their hearts so that they will not depart from Me.

Jeremiah 32:40

The Body in which Jesus chose to tabernacle with mankind, fashioned over two thousand years to be His dwelling place, is Israel, *"...the Word was made flesh* (Jewish flesh) *and dwelt among us"* (John 1.14, the Greek word for dwelt means to tabernacle).

A correct understanding of Israel's significance in the whole counsel of God, summed up in His Son, and the prominence of Israel's place as the key element in the completion of God's purposes on earth, is necessary for our participation in the Father's work of preparing the world for His Son's second

The Blueprint – The Bride of Christ

coming. God has intricately woven all the events surrounding the return of Jesus to the land of Israel, to His work of the restoration of His chosen people. God in the mystery of His wisdom, saw fit to transform Israel's loss into riches for the world:

> *"But if their transgression means riches for the world, and their loss means riches for the Gentiles, how much greater riches will their fullness bring!...For if their rejection is reconciliation of the world, what will their acceptance be but life from the dead?" Romans 11:12 NIV*

> *"For, brothers I want you to understand this truth which God formerly concealed but now has revealed, so that you won't imagine that you know more than you do. It is that stoniness, to a degree, has come upon Israel, until the Gentile world enters in its fullness; and that it is in this way that all Israel will be saved. As the Tanakh says, "Out of Tzion will come the Redeemer; He will turn away ungodliness from Ya'akov and this will be My covenant with them,...when I take away their sins." Romans 11:25 JNT*

Do Gentile believers fully comprehend the price Israel has paid, and continues to pay, for giving the world the gift of God's Word and the gift of His Son Jesus? Can anyone fully fathom on this side of eternity the extent of Israel's sacrifice and the riches the world has received because of Israel's loss?

A large percentage of believer's attitudes, ranging from indifference to hatred of the Jewish people, prove otherwise. Nevertheless, God in the mystery of His wisdom transforms the evil the enemy intended into great blessing!

When Paul states in the above scripture, *"How much greater riches will their fullness bring,"* he is referring to the blessing that the world and believers will

The Blueprint – The Bride of Christ

once again receive when Israel is accepted in Christ and restored to their Father's embrace. He is referring to the massive explosion of God's goodness and blessing the world and believers will again receive when Israel receives the fullness of the Son of God, and He returns to rule and reign over the world.

> *"For the earth will be filled With the knowledge of the glory of the LORD, As the waters cover the sea." Habakkuk 2:14*

The answer to this question of how great will the riches be from Israel's fullness, can be found in the significance of the Greek word *pleroma*, translated also as 'fullness' in verses 12 and 25. The word *pleroma* is defined as, *to fill up, what is filled (as a container), and completion.* The name Israel, which means *prince of God*, is the vessel and prepared body of *Jeshua* that believers have been placed in, stated verse 17. Gentile believers have been grafted into the Olive tree that is Israel, with and among the Jewish people, "...***until** the fullness of the Gentiles has come in*" verse 25.

Israel has been blinded only for a season, **until** the entity that is Israel attains fullness and completion, the fullness of believing Gentiles comes in, and Israel and the Gentile church has entered into a true and authentic union. What are the implications of this 'fullness' and completeness for Israel? The *kairos* time, when the fullness of the Gentiles comes in, will be characterized by the fullness of the Son of God. Jesus will permeate and fill the whole vessel or Body with the fullness of His Life, His Presence and the full measure of the Holy Spirit.

The Blueprint – The Bride of Christ

Jesus' first entrance to earth was to the body of Israel, His second entrance will once again be to the vessel that is Israel:

> *"On that day his feet will stand on the Mount of Olives, east of Jerusalem, and the Mount of Olives will be split in two from east to west, forming a great valley." Zechariah 14:4*

The glorious result of Israel's fullness and completion will be, *"The Deliverer will come from Zion and turn away godlessness from Israel"*—*"And so all Israel will be saved"* (Rom. 11:26).

Paul's use of this Old Testament Scripture in reference to the last days reveals that the Deliverer will make His entrance on planet earth through the Beautiful Gate of Israel once again. God is not finished with Israel as some would purport. All movements of God flow from the River of Life, the Headwaters forever established in Jerusalem on the Day of Pentecost. God cannot lie, and His promises to Israel are yes and Amen!

> *"Thus says the LORD, Who gives the sun for a light by day, the ordinances of the moon and the stars for a light by night, who disturbs the sea, and its waves roar (The LORD of hosts is His name):"If those ordinances depart From before Me, says the LORD then the seed of Israel shall also cease from being a nation before Me forever." Jeremiah 31:35 NIV*

Mounting up with the Lord and moving into the realms of His Glory, is the longing of saints who are passionate for their King. God has been revealing many keys to attain to this place of Glory, however, the most significant key the body has been missing, is the Key of David that opens and no one can shut, spoken of in Isaiah 22:22. This key is a blessing **forever linked to**

The Blueprint – The Bride of Christ

Israel through David, who was representative of Jesus, as the Jewish King of Israel.

Those who choose to receive and honor Israel's place as the fathers, are given *this Key* that opens the gates to all the fullness of God's Glory to the Body of Christ—a gate that no man or demon can shut.

The Tabernacle of David holds all the fullness of God and covers all aspects of Christ, as it embodies the King's Sovereign rule over all facets of the kingdom. The throne of Israel is revealed in the Word of God as the Throne of the Kingdom of the Lord over the Israel of God.

> *"And of all my sons (for the LORD has given me many sons) He has chosen my son Solomon to sit on the throne of the kingdom of the LORD over Israel." 1Chronicles 28:4-5*

"Behold, I will send you Elijah the prophet before the

coming of the great and dreadful day of the LORD.

And he will turn the hearts of the fathers to the children,

And the hearts of the children to their fathers,

Lest I come and strike the earth with a curse."

Malachi 4:6

Honoring the fathers

They will live in the land I gave to my servant Jacob, the land where your fathers lived. They and their children and their children's children will live there forever, and David my servant will be their prince forever. I will make a covenant of peace with them; it will be an everlasting covenant. I will establish them and increase their numbers, and I will put my sanctuary among them forever. My dwelling place will be with them; I will be their God, and they will be my people. Then the nations will know that I the LORD make Israel holy, when my sanctuary is among them forever.'" Ezekiel 37:25-28 (NIV)

Hastening the Day—Honoring the Fathers

What will the acceptance of Israel look like and what will their fullness bring to the world? Moreover, to whom is the promise given of *"life from the dead"* in Romans 11:15? By taking the passages in Romans as a whole, I believe the restoration of Israel to their place and purpose in the Father's plan, and their acceptance by Gentile believers, will result in Resurrection life from the dead for the Body of Christ and a massive worldwide awakening! As a result of the threefold union of Jesus, Israel and Gentile believers, the power of resurrection Life in Christ Jesus, the Head, will be released through His Body. Because of this a New Man will arise in Glory with power to rule and reign over the kingdoms of the earth (Rev. 2:26, Eph. 2:15).

"Life from the dead" is the Body's reception of the fullness of its salvation, released in resurrection power. This will not occur until the importance of Israel's place in the completion of God's plan is understood, Israel is embraced and honored as the fathers of the Church, and restoration begins.

In recent times there has been much revelation and teaching in the body of Christ concerning honoring the fathers. This movement is initiated by the Holy Spirit, to shepherd all who belong to God, into a union of the Body of Christ, that is holy and pure. This movement of honoring the fathers is leading the Body toward this union, and is purposed to find its completion in the restoration of Israel, who are the fathers of Christ, and the fathers Body of Christ.

> *"Who are the Israelites, to whom pertain the adoption, the glory, the covenants, the giving of the law, the service of God and the promises; of*

The Blueprint – The Bride of Christ

whom are the fathers and from whom, according to the flesh Christ came, who is over all, the eternal blessed God. Amen." Romans 9:4-5

All divisions in the Body of Christ that have taken place through the centuries, beginning with the separation from Israel, are now being giving the opportunity for healing and reconciliation that will lead us progressively toward reconciliation with Israel once again.

It is imperative that there be a vital and authentic union between Jew and Gentile—one that produces a New Man, working for the ultimate good and purposes of Christ, to usher in His return to Zion. Through such a union established in honor born of love, the world will then know that the Father sent His Son Jesus into the world for the salvation of mankind (John 17:20).

The union of Israel and the Church is the final breach to be closed for union in the Body of Christ to be complete. God's end-time plans require the closure of this breach, the result of which will be a massive explosion of outpouring of His blessing. In order to close this breach, we must first look at where the breach first occurred and why.

The first division in the church took place when the Roman church took the opportunity to split away from Israel—*the father's of the Church,* in a dispute over the date of the Passover Feast; this decision was made at the Council of Nicea in A.D. 325:

"From the Letter of the Emperor [Constantine] to all those not present at the council (Eusebius Vita Cons., Lib, III, 18-20):

When the question relative to the sacred festival arose, it was universally thought that it would be convenient that all should keep the feast on one day; for what could be more desirable than to see this festival, through which we receive the hope of immortality, celebrated by all with one accord and in the same manner? It was declared to be particularly unworthy for this, the holiest of festivals, to follow the customs of the Jews, who had soiled their hands with the most fearful of crimes, and whose minds were blinded. In rejecting their customs we may transmit to our descendants the legitimate mode of celebrating Easter; which we have observed from the time of the Savior's passion (according to the day of the week).

We ought not therefore to have anything in common with the Jew, for the Savior has shown us another way; our worship following a more legitimate and more convenient course (the order of the days of the week): And consequently in unanimously adopting this mode, we desire, brethren, to separate ourselves from the detestable company of the Jew.

For it is truly shameful for us to hear them boast that without direction we could not keep the feast. How can they be in the right, they who, after the death of the Savior, have no longer been lead by reason but by wild violence, as their delusion may urge them?...

But even if this were not so, It would still be your duty not to tarnish your soul by communication with such wicked people [the Jews]. You should consider not only that the number of churches in these provinces make a majority, but also that it is right to demand that our reason approves, and that we should have nothing in common with the Jews, (The Nicean and Post-Nicean Fathers, Vol. XIV, William B. Eerdsman Publishing Company, 1979, pgs. 54-55).

The Blueprint – The Bride of Christ

The Roman Catholic Church has since made peace with Israel through the Vatican II conclave concerning replacement theology—the belief that the Church has replaced Israel, and through Pope John Paul II's visit to Israel in March 2000, where he apologized to Israel and prayed at the Wailing Wall. Our intention in quoting this document is by no means meant to bring disrepute on our Roman Catholic brothers and sisters.

However, this document became the initiation of the first division within the Body of Christ; a Body that is holy and precious to the Lord, for whom He gave His very Life. Jesus went to the Cross so that the dividing walls could be removed in His sacrificial love, that the two might become One New Man *and* a Holy Bride prepared for His everlasting possession.

The Word of God has shown that Jesus will not return until this breach is repaired, and all things have been restored to the Blueprint established by God from the foundation of the world—declared to us in His Word.

> *"...and that He may send Jesus Christ, who was preached to you before, whom heaven must receive until **the times of restoration of all things,** which God has spoken by the mouth of all His holy prophets since the world began." Acts 3:20-21*

The Greek Word used in this Scripture as restoration is *apokatastasis,* which means *reconstitution* or *restitution*. The definition of reconstitution is to *reconstruct;* this word also means *to return from a dehydrated state to a liquid stated by adding water.* Restitution means *the restoration of rights, or property previously taken away; restoration to the former or original state or position*. It also means, *recompense, make amends and compensate*.

The Blueprint – The Bride of Christ

Before the return of Christ, the Father will see to it that the House of God is reconstructed and restored to His original intention, in obedience to the commands given in His Word. With the outpouring of the water of His Word and the outpouring of the Holy Spirit, the dehydrated Body of Christ will be restored to Life.

God commanded that *His Feasts* were to be held on certain dates, as these dates were significantly related to specific purposes and events. *The date of the Passover Feast, and all seven Feasts, were established by God in the Word of God for specific reasons, and are unchangeable.*

> *"Speak to the children of Israel, and say to them: 'The feasts of the LORD, which you shall proclaim to be holy convocations, these are My feasts... 'These are the feasts of the LORD, holy convocations which you shall proclaim at their appointed times. On the fourteenth day of the first month at twilight is the LORD's Passover." Leviticus 23:2-5*

Jesus *"our Passover"* (1Cor.5:7), was crucified on a specific date ordained by God—*during the Passover Feast*, signifying the end of the dispensation of Law, and our Passover into the dispensation of Grace. The outpouring of the Holy Spirit also fell on a specific date ordained by God—fifty days after Passover, *at the Feast of Pentecost*. Because God ordained specific dates to hold each of His Feasts, it is only reasonable to expect that the dates for the feasts yet to be fulfilled, are also important and vital in His purposes, as His plans continue to unfold.

The Gentile church has chosen to change the Passover to a time called Easter—a pagan festival; this has therefore changed the date of Pentecost which was to be held fifty days later. God has been very merciful and gracious, and has even had His purposes in allowing the Gentile church to change the dates of His Feasts, *for a season*.

As *'the fullness of the Gentiles comes in'* to Israel, and as we approach the end of the age—the time of the summing up of all things in Christ and the restoration of all things—it will become increasingly important for the Body of Christ to honor the dates ordained by God the Father.

There are many good reasons for restoration to the original dates; first and foremost, to honor God's Word and restore things to *His* order, and secondly, to honor Israel, to *"turn the hearts of the children to the fathers and the fathers to the children."* The restoration of the original dates will be an important act in the healing and closing of the breach between Israel and the Gentile Church, and will facilitate the union of both in Christ—*our Passover*.

God will send His servants in the spirit of Elijah to prepare the way of the Lord, and turn the heart of the fathers to the children and the children to the fathers. The consequences of disobedience to God's will is dire for us and for the world—*"lest I strike the earth with a curse"* (Mal.4:6).

We can hasten the day of the Lord's return by honoring and loving the Jewish people for the price they have paid, working with the Lord to see them restored and established in the fullness of their calling, praying and interceding for them, and supporting them as we are admonished to, *"For if the Gentiles have shared in the Jews' spiritual blessings, they owe it to the Jews to share with them their material blessings"* (Romans 15:26-27).

The Blueprint – The Bride of Christ

"By Abolishing in His [own crucified] flesh the enmity [caused by]

The Law with its decrees and ordinances [which He annulled];

That He from the two might create in Himself one new man

[One new quality of humanity out of the two], so masking peace.

And [He designed] to reconcile to God both

[Jew and Gentile, united] in a single body by means of His cross,

Thereby killing the mutual enmity and bringing the feud to an end."

Ephesians 2:15-16 AMP

One United

Christine Peterkin

Since establishing His Church in Christ on the foundation of Israel, God has been at work in the Gentile nations, for two thousand years. This may seem like a very long time, and may have given the impression that God is finished with Israel, but a thousand years is a day to the Lord. God is now making the necessary preparations to move into the final phase of His work, where His eyes are centered on Israel, as Israel awakens once again to their

The Blueprint – The Bride of Christ

God. Jesus became a stumbling block to Israel, but Israel has also become a stumbling block to the Church. In this last phase of His work, He will remove the veil of blindness from Israel's eyes, and from the eyes of the Gentile church concerning Israel and there will be a great Awakening. At the time that the Foundation was laid and the Cornerstone, there was a great invasion of earth by Heaven, releasing great signs and wonders; the establishment of the Headstone and the release of the 'sons of God' will also come with a great invasion of earth and great signs in the Heavens and earth.

Israel is a both a natural and spiritual entity, a vessel that is progressively being transformed by God, from the natural into a Heavenly City (Gen. 22:17). Many look at Jerusalem with natural eyes and all they can see is a bloody City; it is time to begin to see with God's eyes; to understand with his heart, His passion for this nation, which has paid such a tremendous cost to be marked with His Name, from their conception to this present day. It is important to challenge our beliefs and examine carefully in the Holy Spirit our doctrine concerning Israel, as Heaven begins to shine Light on the Word, releasing fresh revelation concerning Israel, for such a time as this.

> *"But now in Christ Jesus you who once were far away have been brought near through the blood of Christ. For he himself is our peace, who has made the two one and has destroyed the barrier, the dividing wall of hostility, by abolishing in his flesh the law with its commandments and regulations. His purpose was to create in himself one new man out of the two, thus making peace..." Ephesians 2:13-15 NIV*

On the Day of Pentecost the disciples who gathered together were in one accord; they were of one mind as they waited to receive the Promise of the

The Blueprint – The Bride of Christ

Father spoken of by Jesus (Acts 1:4). Because of the unity amongst them, the disciples were positioned to receive the commanded blessing (Acts 1:14 2:1). God will command His blessing when there is union in His body.

> *"Behold, how good and how pleasant it is for brethren to dwell together in unity! It is like the precious oil upon the head, running down on the beard, the beard of Aaron, Running down on the edge of his garments. It is like the dew of Hermon, descending upon the mountains of Zion; for there the LORD commanded the blessing— Life forevermore." Psalm 133*

God's view of union is portrayed by oil flowing down from the Head of Aaron—the high priest of Israel, down his beard to the edge of his priestly garments. Union of the Body of Christ cannot be accomplished until there is union Between Israel and the Gentile church, and Israel is restored to the place of the head and not the tail. The River flows from Heaven through Jerusalem, and the oil flows from the Head of Christ through Israel to His Body.

The Lord's ultimate plan is that the Gentile Church work together with the Jewish servants of God, to see Israel restored and prepared as the Bride for her coming Bridegroom and King, *"...make straight in the desert a highway for our God"* (Isaiah 40:3).

> *"For I tell you that Christ has become a servant of the Jews on behalf of God's truth, to confirm the promises made to the patriarchs so that the Gentiles may glorify God for his mercy, as it is written: "Therefore I will praise you among the Gentiles; I will sing hymns to your name." Again, it says, "Rejoice, O Gentiles, with his people." Romans 15:8-12*

The Blueprint – The Bride of Christ

To everything, there is a season and a time for every purpose; the time has come for Jew and Gentile to work together to build the Temple of the Lord according to God's blueprint, and to bring in the Ark of His Presence.

In the same way that David made all the preparation and provisions for the building of the Temple of God, Jesus has made all the preparations and provision for the Temple to be completed. The stones have been prepared, the wood has been cut, the iron for the doors and gates is ready, and there is bronze, silver and gold in abundance, and the wine and the oil is prepared (1 Chronicles 22).

God has been at work preparing His skilled workers—Intercessors, leaders, churches and ministries; specialists in every field of building work, *"all types of skillful men"* and women, each one having their part to contribute, important the completion of the House.

The wine and the oil are being prepared to be poured out, to sustain and equip all the workers to complete the building, and for the procession to bring the Ark of His Presence into the Sanctuary.

> *"Now set your heart and your soul to seek the LORD your God. Therefore arise and build the sanctuary of the LORD God, to bring the ark of the covenant of the LORD and the holy articles of God into the house that is to be built for the name of the LORD." 1Chronicles:22:19*

The enemies of God have been uniting against the Kingdom of God and have been gaining ground. The Body of Christ has proven to be very weak because of its many divisions. It is time to set our focus on the Father and submission to the Father's Will and the Father's ways, as the fullness of time for *the*

The Blueprint – The Bride of Christ

Father's purposes and *the Father's* dreams has come. As Victor Hugo once said, *"Like the trampling of a mighty army, such is the force of an idea whose time has come."*

We are now approaching the time for the Father's dream of the completion of His House—the building of the Headstone; the time of the Father's dream for his daughters; the time of the revelation of the Sons of God; the time of the restoration of all things.

It is time for the fullness of the Father's Promise—*the commanded blessing*; the time of the *Day of His Power*—when His people volunteer freely. It is time for the day of the Harvest—the day of multitudes of harvesters being sent into the fields to bless the world in the Spirit of the Father.

It is time for the restoration of the nation of Israel and the Jewish people; the time for love and union in the Body of Christ, the time to end the night of wrong as stated by the poet William Merrill:

Rise up, O men of God! Have done with lesser things;
Give heart and mind and soul and strength to serve the King of Kings.
Rise up O men of God! His Kingdom tarries long;
Bring in the day of brotherhood and end the night of wrong.
Rise up O men of God!
The Church for you doth wait,
Her strength unequal to her task
RISE UP AND
MAKE HER GREAT!

The Blueprint – Appendix

Prophecies Concerning Israel

"Behold, I will send and take all the families of the north,' says the LORD, 'and Nebuchadnezzar the king of Babylon, my servant, and will bring them against this land, against its inhabitants, and against these nations all around, and will utterly destroy them, and make them an astonishment, a hissing, and perpetual desolations...And this whole land shall be a desolation and an astonishment, and these nations shall serve the king of Babylon seventy years. Then it will come to pass, when seventy years are completed, that I will punish the king of Babylon and that nation, the land of the Chaldeans, for their iniquity,' says the LORD; 'and I will make it a perpetual desolation." Jeremiah 25:9

"'They shall be carried to Babylon, and there they shall be until the day that I visit them,' says the LORD. Then I will bring them up and restore them to this place." Jeremiah 27:22

"Since you were precious in My sight, you have been honored, and I have loved you; Therefore I will give men for you, And people for your life. Fear not, for I am with you; I will bring your descendants from the east, and gather you from the west; I will say to the north, 'Give them up!' And to the south, 'Do not keep them back!' Bring My sons from afar, And My daughters from the ends of the earth—Everyone who is called by My name, whom I have created for My glory; I have formed him, yes, I have made him." Isaiah 43:4-7

"Then Jesus went out and departed from the temple, and His disciples came up to show Him the buildings of the temple. And Jesus said to them, "Do you not see all these things? Assuredly, I say to you, not one stone shall be left here upon another, that shall not be thrown down." Matthew 24:1-2

"It shall come to pass in that day that the Lord shall set His hand again the second time to recover the remnant of His people who are left, from Assyria and Egypt, from Pathros and Cush, from Elam and Shinar, from Hamath and the islands of the sea. He will set up a banner for the nations, and will assemble the outcasts of Israel, and gather together the dispersed of Judah from the four corners of the earth." Isaiah 11:11

"Therefore behold, the days are coming," says the LORD, "that it shall no more be said, 'The LORD lives who brought up the children of Israel from the land of Egypt,' but, 'The LORD lives who brought up the children of Israel from the land of the north and from all the lands where

The Blueprint — Appendix

He had driven them.' For I will bring them back into their land which I gave to their fathers. Jeremiah 16:14-15

"On that day I will raise up The tabernacle of David, which has fallen down, and repair its damages; I will raise up its ruins, and rebuild it as in the days of old; that they may possess the remnant of Edom, and all the Gentiles who are called by My name," Says the LORD who does this thing." Amos 9:11-12

"For behold, in those days and at that time, when I bring back the captives of Judah and Jerusalem, I will also gather all nations, and bring them down to the Valley of Jehoshaphat; And I will enter into judgment with them there on account of My people, My heritage Israel, whom they have scattered among the nations; they have also divided up My land." Joel 3:1-2

Related Scripture: Ezekiel 20:40-44, 34:11-30, 37:1-28, Isaiah 60:8-16, Hosea 3, 4, 5

Headstone Ministries

1-312 Reynolds Street

Oakville ON Canada

L6J 3L8

Website: www.headstoneministries.com
Email: contact@headstoneministries.com

One United painting by Christine Peterkin – www.inspirationalart.ca
Israel My Son illustration by Martha Charlton

Publications in the Yahweh's House Series:

Faith Baczko is available to teach seminars based on any of the publications in the *Yahweh's House Series*

The Plumb Line – 'The Christ'
A Journey of Freedom and Deliverance!

The Blueprint – 'The Messiah'
God's Transcendent plan of Redemption!

In Our Image – 'The Christ'
...And Female He Created, for Such a Time!

Soon to be released in the Series:

The Headstone – 'The Christ'
If We Build It, He Will Return!

Israel My Son – Prince of God
I have Loved Thee with an Everlasting Love!

Yahweh – LORD of Armies
The Warfare of Heaven, In the Day of His Power!

The Bride – 'The Christ'
"Come, and I will show You the Bride"

The Blueprint is available on CD as a Power Point Presentation with narration. Visit our website for more information.

Our books are also available at -

Catch the Fire Resources, amazon .com, amazon.ca,

Made in the USA
Charleston, SC
19 May 2011